INCLUSIVE TEACHING

TEACHING AND LEARNING IN HIGHER EDUCATION
James M. Lang, Series Editor
Michelle D. Miller, Series Editor

A list of titles in this series appears at the end of this volume.

INCLUSIVE TEACHING

Strategies for
Promoting Equity in the
College Classroom

Kelly A. Hogan and Viji Sathy

West Virginia University Press
Morgantown

ISBN 978-1-952271-63-2 (paperback) / 978-1-952271-64-9 (ebook)

Library of Congress Cataloging-in-Publication Data is available
from the Library of Congress

Cover design by Than Saffel / WVU Press

*To all the educators, overworked and underpaid,
who never stop thinking about their students.*

CONTENTS

——

PREFACE

We met in a cramped conference room with a group of ten colleagues in a faculty learning community hosted by the teaching and learning center on our campus. One of our assignments was to observe each other teaching and then meet to discuss our pedagogy. Debriefing over coffee, we immediately identified many ideas we held in common: we were both feeling dissatisfied with aspects of our courses and we felt frustrated that being a funny, dynamic lecturer seemed to be the definition of effective teaching by students and colleagues. We didn't see how an instructor's personality equated to effective learning. Discovering we were both introverts, we affirmed each other's thoughts that deep learning by students shouldn't require us to become people we are not. We had discussions about what pedagogical strategies better fit our personalities and the intended student outcomes. If only Jessamyn Neuhaus, author of *Geeky Pedagogy: A Guide for Intellectuals, Introverts, and Nerds Who Want to Be Effective Teachers,* had published her book earlier, we surely would have added it to the reading list for the faculty learning community. In her book, Neuhaus takes exception to "any hint of a suggestion that effective teaching requires a specific kind of innate personality quality or emotional state, rather than being a set of skills, attitudes, actions, abilities, and a reflective, intellectual approach that can be learned, applied, and improved with effort by anyone who wants to be an effective teacher" (Neuhaus, 2019, p. 5).

Frustration and introversion were not our only commonalities. Like so many instructors in higher education, neither of us had much pedagogy training in our graduate programs. Early in our careers, teaching workshops and education-based literature made big impressions on our development. Both scientists by training, we approached making changes to our courses through a scientific and data-driven lens. We believed that we could continually improve our abilities with teaching, a belief Carol Dweck defines as a growth mind-set (Dweck, 2006). We assumed then, and still today, that effective teaching is a challenge that requires hard work, intent, practice, mistakes, reflection, and iteration. It was never a problem for us to admit to ourselves and each other when we faced challenges in our own teaching. Often, the first step to making change is to recognize that a problem exists. Because of our mind-sets and generally optimistic, change-maker attitudes, we embraced our teaching challenges and set out to overcome them.

As we bounced ideas back and forth, we discovered we were quite compatible. We continued to give each other feedback through class observations and we spent more time together through campus committees, grant work, and various meetings. We often discussed what we saw as shortfalls in inclusivity with our experiences in colleagues' classrooms, at university meetings that lacked good facilitation, and at campus-wide events. Slowly, our ideas formed into the basis of workshops for colleagues and articles we wanted to write. This book represents what we have learned from our own experiences as practicing educators, from our dive into the scholarship of teaching and learning, and from what we've learned by exchanging ideas with colleagues locally and afar.

An important lesson we have learned is that language is always evolving. For example, we used to use the term *underrepresented minority* (URM) to include Black, Latinx, and Indigenous people. We now use the word *minoritized* in place of URM. This terminology shifts away from characteristics that are socially constructed and recognizes systemic barriers and oppression that have characterized particular groups (Sotto-Santiago, 2019). Similarly, we took a look at the phrase *achievement gap*, which is used in a lot of the educational research literature, including our own. In a radio interview, Ibram X. Kendi points out that the term achievement gap can be interpreted to mean that lower achievement is due to some deficit in minoritized students (Hahn, 2019). When describing past research studies that used the term, we simply tried to explain the disparities. In other places we chose the term opportunity gap, which Kendi better describes as "what the problem is and thereby what the solution is."

Another term we use in this book to refers to students who do not enter school speaking only English. In some contexts, this group of students may be referred to as English as Second Language (ESL) learners or English as Primary Language (EPL) learners to indicate another language may be first or equal in use for a student. We choose to use the term *multilingual* to describe those who enter a US school speaking a language other than English as their primary language at home (as opposed to *monolingual*—students enter school speaking only English). English learners are multilingual students who may have not yet mastered English. We chose the term multilingual to not only decenter English, but to favor the strengths-based orientation of speaking multiple languages.

We recognize that some of the language that we choose

today will continue to evolve. Language naturally changes as people wrestle with words that feel more inclusive to the people and experiences they describe.

There is a familiar story that has been adapted many times over and anchors our beliefs as educators. Below is a version inspired by "The Star Thrower," by Loren C. Eiseley:

> After an ocean storm, hundreds of starfish washed up on a long beach. A man walking along the beach sees a young girl throwing one starfish at a time into the water. The man is amused by her and watches her for a while. Eventually he approaches her. Smiling, he says, "There are so many starfish, you can't save them all! You can barely make a difference!" The girl stares at him for a moment. She takes a deep breath and picks up another starfish. She turns to him and with a smile, she throws the starfish back into the sea. She tells him, "I made a difference to that one." As she picks up another she says, "And that one too!"

We both keep email folders with unsolicited comments from our "starfish," telling us how we helped them individually. Many students articulate feelings of belonging and inclusion, often for the first time in a college classroom. Reading these makes us feel the importance of our work as educators. They remind us of the role we play in truly welcoming students into our disciplines and helping all students succeed. We do not want to be considered gatekeepers who keep students out.

We are not alone. Many educators are looking through the lens of equity and determining that they need more inclusive teaching strategies. If you are an educator, we invite you to continually reflect on your role not merely as someone who equips students with knowledge and skills, but also as an architect of environments for inclusive learning and experiences. We can all promote and model inclusive experiences in our meetings, workshops, and trainings.

It is our hope that by reading this book and reflecting on your practices, you pick up practical tips you can use to immediately refine your work. We are practitioners at heart and thus our writing often feels like an advice guide we would have benefited from when we got our start in education nearly twenty-five years ago. We have suggested many tips (a whole book's worth!) and we encourage you to consider what you might like to prioritize in getting started. We don't expect that you will be able to dive into every tip in a single term. It took us many years to learn and implement these principles; we are still uncovering our own areas for improvement. Adopting an inclusive teaching mind-set is recognizing that you are not working toward one end goal. Inclusion is a continual journey. We have written this book to support you on this journey by providing a framework and common language we can share. Let's continue to learn together and help many more starfish reach the ocean!

CHAPTER 1

INCLUSIVE TEACHING AS A MIND-SET

In 2009, a colleague at the campus teaching and learning center shared a spreadsheet with Kelly about how students were doing in large introductory science courses. Although the data were not identified by faculty, Kelly was one of only two primary instructors of Biology 101. Her eyes darted to that section of the table. Her heart sank as she immediately felt ownership of the data. These kinds of data were rarely seen by instructors at the time, before the sophisticated data analytics tools that more faculty have access to now.

The data showed that in the introductory biology course Black students were more likely to earn grades of D and F compared to white or Asian students, similar to trends first noticed by Uri Treisman in the late 1970s (Treisman, 1992). She was also aware of retention issues for all students interested in STEM but especially those from traditionally marginalized groups. National data around this time showed that only about 15 percent of the Latinx, Black, and Native American students who intended to major in science actually graduated with a degree in science in four years (Hurtado,

Eagan, & Chang, 2010). She had never considered these kinds of data relative to her own teaching and her students. Reflecting on both her own and national data for the first time caused Kelly to realize that she might be contributing to the national problem and limiting who had access to becoming a scientist. She often describes the experience of seeing the data as a punch in the gut because it was not in line with her philosophy of education or her vision of equity. Despite external validation from students and colleagues, Kelly began to question her own teaching effectiveness. Could she consider herself an effective teacher with such large differences in student outcomes by demographics? The genie could not be put back in the bottle.

Like Kelly, Viji was struggling with patterns she was observing in her own class in introductory statistics. Over and over, students were introducing themselves to Viji privately in office hours and after class with a common phrase: "I just wanted to let you know that I am not a math person." This sentiment was at odds with Viji's mind-set. She believed that all students who had arrived in her classroom had the ability to succeed in the course. After all, they gained admittance to the institution and completed the necessary prerequisites. She believed in the power of practice because she knew it firsthand. During high school, she struggled with math. She worked nightly on her homework with her father, who loved math. To help coach Viji through challenging problems, her father relearned much of the content. Gradually, Viji became one of the few students in her math class who found solutions to the hardest problems. The practice and payoff helped her develop confidence and, ultimately, a love of quantitative reasoning. Viji suspected the attitudes of many of her students were shaped by prior negative quantitative experiences, but they didn't have the opportunity to reshape their experiences with at-home coaching like she had. She wanted to convince students that, with effort, they all were capable of succeeding.

Viji noted another troubling, related issue. She saw a diverse group of learners in her classroom in terms of gender, ethnicity, and many other characteristics. Yet when she attended professional conferences in her discipline, there seemed to be limited participation by individuals with these characteristics. Retention issues in STEM were made real for her when she compared her classroom and professional events. How could she increase participation in her discipline when success in quantitative disciplines like statistics seemed unattainable to so many students?

The experiences we've described were pivotal moments for the two authors of this book. They led us to recognize that we wanted to improve equity and inclusion issues in our classrooms and, ultimately, our disciplines. Yet it felt overwhelming to think about how to approach these problems. Like many instructors, we tried some innovative ideas, made changes based on feedback from students and peers, and further refined our thinking. Over time, we began to see the gaps in our own teaching in many places. Specifically, we recognized we could do better with inclusion. This book is a window into what we noticed, what we've tried, and what we've learned, along with some practical ideas we hope readers will adapt for their corners of the educational world.

Can We Change Our Pedagogy and Meet the Needs of More Students?

We find it to be an exciting time to be teaching in higher education. Our classrooms are more diverse than ever, with more students of color, first-generation students, students from low-income backgrounds, full-time workers, and those who balance college courses with parenting duties (American Council on Education, 2019, Chapter 3). This diversity has the potential to change society for the better. However, systemic barriers are preventing some of the underrepresented groups in our classrooms from reaching their full potential.

Unfortunately, some educators have responded to this rapid shift in demographics by blaming students for arriving to our classrooms with different resources, experiences, cultures, or values. This sentiment is evident in statements we've heard firsthand from faculty, such as "students don't know how to read anymore." But we emphatically state that diversity is not a problem. In fact, there's growing literature about the positive impact of diverse teams on problem-solving and teamwork (Phillips, 2014; Rock & Grant, 2016). When we pause to reflect about the value of a diverse population of students, most of us likely appreciate the variety of perspectives our students bring into the classroom.

The often implicit belief that some students are deficient hinders our collective ability to make education an equalizer. It is simply not enough that our institutions accept a more diverse group if everyone doesn't play a role in ensuring the success of all students. Success takes into account feelings of inclusion and goals of equity.

Let's define three principal words relative to our students: diversity, equity, and inclusion.

- Diversity describes the ways students are similar and different from one another. A diverse population doesn't mean the learning environment is automatically inclusive.
- Equity is the goal we strive to reach, in which all learners start by having access to the same opportunities. But access is not enough. Equity requires naming and dismantling the

systems, structures, and oppressive forces that act as barriers for some students more than others. When we work to remove barriers, more individuals can succeed. This is an ongoing process.

- Inclusion describes a culture in which all learners feel welcome, valued, and safe, and it requires intentional and deliberate strategies.

We have plenty of evidence about how to improve learning for students who have been traditionally underserved, undervalued, and excluded in higher education. Some of the solutions are outside of an instructor's control, such as a lack of bus fare or a stressful roommate situation. These issues are better addressed by staff in financial aid or student affairs. Yet educators can play a significant role in student retention and success by choosing to utilize inclusive teaching strategies. Adopting these strategies often means intentionally moving away from how instructors were traditionally taught. While change by educators requires time, knowledge, encouragement, and courage, we have both personally found our journey toward inclusion and equity in our classes to be empowering. We, as instructors, can celebrate student diversity and leverage it to enhance learning. We can ensure that more of our students successfully reach their goals. Through this lens of empowerment, let's look at some of the changes we each made in our courses once we observed the troubling patterns described in the opening pages of this chapter.

How Did Kelly Make Changes?

Recall that Kelly had observed large discrepancies in achievement in her introductory biology course based on race and ethnicity. At the time, she had an instructor-centered approach. Students spent most of their time in class taking notes while she lectured. Kelly looked for solutions that would align with how all students learn. For her more than 400 students (and no TAs in the course with her), she needed to find a structure that would increase low-stakes practice with skills and concepts in biology. Yet she believed that if the practice was going to reach the students that needed it most, it could not be optional. The increased practice would help the students who needed it without harming the students who already knew how to learn on their own.

Kelly also felt that whatever new approaches she adopted would need to include immediate feedback to students, so they could self-assess often and accurately before high-stakes exams. Because the students far outnumbered her, Kelly sought out technologies that could help her reach these goals. She thought she could level the playing field by requiring all students to do pre-class homework. Kelly changed the course design by adding guided reading questions and required reading assessment questions twice a week, through an online homework platform that provided hints, tutorials, and animations. A variety of active learning experiences during class time included required participation through a classroom response system and many opportunities to collaborate.

In sum, Kelly began teaching a more highly structured course. Because structure is a word we will continually come back to, let's clarify the difference between low- and high-structure courses as defined by Scott Freeman et al. (Freeman, Haak, & Wenderoth, 2011)

- Low-structure courses have traditional lectures with only a few high-stakes assessments, such as two midterm exams and a final exam.
- Highly structured courses "assign daily and weekly active-learning exercises with the goal of providing constant

practice with the analytical skills required to do well on exams" (Freeman, Haak, & Wenderoth, 2011).

Kelly collected survey and performance data on her students before and after she created a more structured course. Early analysis of the data suggested a disproportionate beneficial impact for certain student groups. She and a colleague, Sarah Eddy, demonstrated that the increased structure helped all students. Differences in performance between Black students and white students were halved and differences between first-generation college students and non-first-generation college students disappeared (Eddy & Hogan, 2014). While evidence was accumulating that active learning was improving overall outcomes in other large STEM courses, Kelly and Sarah's publication, with disaggregated data, was one of the first to demonstrate how this kind of change in pedagogy could benefit traditionally underrepresented student groups even more than other groups. The study received attention in the national mainstream media, with articles in the *New York Times* and the *Atlantic*. In subsequent semesters, Kelly continued to see the narrowing of differences in the performance of traditionally underrepresented students by refining her approach and bringing even more structure to her course. She felt compelled to share with others the difference and impact one educator could make.

One student sent Kelly an email that sums up that good feeling a teacher can have knowing their goals were accomplished on some level:

"I want to take a moment to thank you deeply for being instrumental in fueling within me a small beam of hope which has been my north star since BIOL 101; that a first-generation college student from a poverty background despite the adversities can do what affluent peers do. My former HS track coach use to say, 'a candle loses nothing by lighting another candle' and I feel that is what you did for me. Thank you."

How Did Viji Make Changes?

In her courses, Viji was observing that many students were self-identifying as "not a math person." This mind-set was likely keeping many students from even thinking a STEM field was for them. She wanted to convey to students that their work ethic could be the main driver of success, not some genetic predisposition to math (Kimball, Smith, & Quartz, 2013). She wanted to increase a sense of belonging and interest in the discipline. She wanted to open doors to disciplines for her students.

Like Kelly, Viji recognized that a lot more practice by students was necessary to reach her goals. However, she discovered that she wasn't using class time well for all students. She had always tried to teach to the middle. When she polled students, she discovered the pacing was "just right" for 40 percent. However, for 20 percent of students it was "slow," and for 40 percent it was "fast" or "too fast." Shooting down the middle was not working for 60 percent of her students. This discovery was at odds with the philosophy she often shared with students: it's not about how fast you understand it, it's about understanding it. She regularly stressed to her students that learning was not a speed contest. The pace was crucial because disparities in comprehension became a challenge to overcome as the semester progressed in a cumulative quantitative course like hers. She wanted to acknowledge that despite differences in learning, all were welcome to statistics.

Viji reasoned that posting short videos of herself solving problems that students were required to watch would allow students to go at their own pace and rewatch videos if needed. The videos would allow students to complete tedious calculations at their own pace before class (what many deemed the boring stuff) and then spend class time doing the more challenging work of applying the concepts to interesting psychological and societal issues.

Viji collected data before and after the changes she made to her teaching. She found significant gains in achievement across the grade distribution, student engagement, perceptions of the course, and interest (Sathy & Moore, 2020). It is noteworthy that for students who have traditionally had lower levels of participation in quantitative disciplines (women and minoritized students), nearly all measures were disproportionately improved. While she doesn't have data about who entered her discipline, student notes like this help her see that she is making a difference with participation.

Before your class, I was TERRIFIED of statistics. You were so patient. So kind. And even though I wasn't one of your "A" students, you never made me feel less than. You were just as frustrated as I was when you knew I knew an answer and the test anxiety would just get to me. It was your determination and your constant encouragement that made me not want to give up. I didn't leave your class with an A but I left your class with actual knowledge of concepts AND I was no longer scared of the big bad statistics class. Now in a PhD program, I will be finishing a quantitative concentration next year. (That's right, I signed up to take 6 statistics classes for FUN.) I'm no longer afraid to ask questions in class and I often ask the most questions (lol) but your class gave me the courage to do so. Thank you for all you do and your prioritizing of meeting students where they are. Even if you don't see the fruits of your labor immediately, I hope you know you are changing lives.

In both of our stories, dissatisfaction with our courses prompted us to change our teaching to align with our vision of equity in educational spaces. Our scientific training led us to want to examine our changes in a measured way. At the same time, we reflected on who we were as undergraduate learners and the methods that would have appealed to students like us and many others. Eventually, our commonalities and discussions led us to the shared solution of inclusive teaching.

What Is Inclusive Teaching?

To better reflect on the word inclusion, we often like to consider the definition of the word *exclude*: "to prevent or restrict the entrance of, to bar from participation, consideration, or inclusion" (Merriam-Webster, 2021). Many of us educators would be aghast at subscribing to tactics that would exclude students, and yet we often unwittingly do so. For example, consider a common occurrence in a classroom where an instructor poses a question and a few hands go up to share a response. The instructor may feel it is inclusive because all were invited to contribute, but not all students do. Our younger selves often felt excluded by this teaching strategy. Inclusion is a culture in which all learners feel welcome, valued, and safe.

When participation relies on volunteers speaking aloud to a group, it is often the same few people that contribute. For example, Jay Howard's work on talker versus nontalker behaviors and perceptions in the classroom makes evident that voluntary participation can lead to a "consolidation of responsibility" (Howard & Baird, 2000) among students. First coined in 1976 by David Karp and William Yoels, the term *consolidation of responsibility* refers to the norm in a typical classroom in which participation in a discussion will be consolidated by the voices of a few, with most students being passive observers or only occasional participants (Karp & Yoels, 1976). Inclusion requires intentional and deliberate strategies. Fortunately, a few small tweaks such as classroom responses systems or small discussion groups can avoid passively excluding most students and actively including all voices. It is our hope that readers of this book will continue to fine-tune their inclusive teaching mind-set and utilize these kinds of small changes in their pedagogy.

By an inclusive teaching mind-set, we mean that every pedagogical decision should be countered with two questions:

1. Who might be left behind as a result of my practice?
2. How can I invite those students in?

We subscribe to a framework developed by Kimberly Tanner, who reasons that when learning environments are unstructured, they can lead to feelings of unfairness, feelings of exclusion, and collisions of students' cultural backgrounds with the learning environment (Tanner, 2017). By adding structure to learning environments we can mitigate unfairness, promote feelings of inclusion, and promote student success.

To concretize the concept of structure further, let's consider two hypothetical students:

Vanessa is a gifted student in a class with a Socratic approach. She's not comfortable raising her hand or blurting out answers the way other students do. She's concerned that the instructor thinks she is not engaged.

Michael is an engaged student who is comfortable in class and in discussions, but he is unexpectedly having a hard time adjusting to the challenges of college. He's feeling like a fraud. Up to this point, he was able to do well by memorizing a lot of content. He's in a course in his major in which the grade is composed of only two midterm papers and one exam. He bombed the exam and he's concerned that he may have chosen the wrong major to pursue.

In both scenarios, these students are likely feeling that they do not belong, and they may be questioning their abilities. Educators have the power to change the narrative in students' minds. Vanessa would benefit from varied and structured opportunities for participation, such as anonymous ways to participate, small-group discussions, or a discussion board assignment. A single method of asking and vocally answering to an entire class is an example of low structure in classroom facilitation. In this low-structure scenario, Vanessa's ideas are not part of the conversation, and others aren't learning from her. She may feel undervalued in this discipline and move away from it. Adding structures that intentionally help a student like Vanessa doesn't harm others. Varied modes of participation help many more students feel comfortable contributing. As a result, a more diverse set of ideas are shared.

As for Michael, he would benefit from more structured practice and frequent feedback. Without multiple opportunities for low-stakes required assessments (such as routine homework and short quizzes), the course is an example of low-structure course design. Michael's talent is not being developed and he may feel like he needs to change majors. This discipline might miss out on an engaged student. Adding more structure in the form of required, frequent practice helps a student like Michael, along with many others.

Plenty of research beyond our own is emerging that

backs up the idea that inclusive teaching strategies can get us closer to our collective goals around equity. One such example is a meta-analysis of published studies in STEM. Researchers found compelling evidence that the kinds of pedagogies that are inclusive (i.e., active learning) reduce differences between minoritized and non-minoritized groups, but only when 67–100 percent of total class time was spent on active learning (Theobald et al., 2020). Thus, this kind of teaching is also an act of antiracism. It was rewarding for us to see that the authors of this large meta-study come to similar conclusions as we have through our many years as practitioners.

In working with many educators and future educators, we find two common misconceptions about inclusive teaching:

- An educator can call their course inclusive once they have incorporated readings and research from a diverse group of scholars.
- Inclusive teaching applies to some disciplines or courses more than others.

Curricular materials created by and about a diverse set of individuals are an important part of inclusive teaching, yet inclusive teaching does not start and end there. Additionally, a course does not need to center on the subject of diversity to be inclusive. Inclusive teaching includes the intentional ways instructors interact with students, provide multiple opportunities to practice the work in a discipline, and demonstrate care. All educators can do these things, so we like to think of inclusive teaching as a mind-set that is discipline-agnostic. One of the most empowering aspects of an inclusive mind-set is that it can be employed by anyone in any educational setting.

We would be remiss if we didn't acknowledge that much of what we discuss in this book has overlapping contexts. One example is universal design for learning (UDL) that emerged in the 1990s through the work of the Center for Applied Special Technology (CAST). Historically, universal design has been perceived by many through the lens of disability service advocacy. Yet at its core, UDL is a framework grounded in neuroscience about human learning and aimed at a broad set of educators who want to strengthen the engagement and performance of all students. We admire the work of Thomas Tobin and Kirsten Behling in their book *Reach Everyone, Teach Everyone: Universal Design for Learning in Higher Education* (Tobin & Behling, 2018). They help a wider audience see that UDL is not about expanding accommodations to more students but is rather a design-thinking mind-set from the outset that benefits all learners. UDL is a component of inclusive teaching and one we are informed by in our writing of this book.

Another overlapping context is trauma-informed pedagogy, which keeps personalized responses to trauma in mind. For example, providing content ahead of time, giving warnings about sensitive content, and building flexibility into assignments are strategies to keep individual students in mind who have experienced trauma (and, importantly, should not need to self-disclose). We find Mays Imad's writing on this topic clarifying, especially as she helped readers relate COVID-19 to other types of trauma our students experience: "The origin of trauma does not have to be violent or abusive, because trauma is centered in an individual experience and can have conscious and unconscious manifestations. Two students may be exposed to the same events but experience those events in vastly different ways, where one student's reality is traumatic while the other's is not"

(Imad, 2020). Like UDL, trauma-informed pedagogy helps shape our own practices and writing.

Similarly, many excellent educators have written pieces and collated resources about inclusive teaching. For example, Brian Dewsbury and Cynthia Brame wrote a piece on inclusive teaching and developed a rich set of inclusive teaching resources for STEM educators with an emphasis on gender, ethnic, and racial diversity (Dewsbury & Brame, 2019). Their framework begins with developing self-awareness and empathy, followed by thinking through issues of classroom environment, managing pedagogical choices, and leveraging networks for inclusion. We find this to be a very informative framework and have utilized it in our own development and writing.

When we both began thinking about the troubling patterns we were observing in our own classrooms, the solutions relied on research into human learning. We wanted to engage our students with evidence-based ideas around practice and learning, and not just *some* students—all students. There are many ways to engage learners that are based on how the brain works. As a starting point, we recommend Joshua Eyler's *How Humans Learn*, Sarah Rose Cavanagh's *The Spark of Learning*, Daniel Willingham's *Why Don't Students Like School?*, and Peter Brown, Henry Roediger, and Mark McDaniel's *Make It Stick* (Eyler, 2018; Cavanagh, 2016; Willingham, 2021; Brown, Roediger, and McDaniel, 2014). At their core, they share a premise of designing with the end goals in mind, using student-centered practice that reflects what we know about cognitive science and emotion, and implementing active learning.

As we began sharing our developing ideas with colleagues outside of STEM, we realized the ideas resonated widely with educators in most disciplines at any stage in their career.

Additionally, by presenting student diversity as a broad range of characteristics, it seemed we were opening a door for some educators to step into the conversation about inclusive teaching for the first time. For example, beyond gender, race, and ethnicity, we often include discussions of students who are first-generation college students, transfer students, multilingual, from low-resource contexts, introverts, immigrants, neurodiverse students, students with mental illness, students who hold unpopular political beliefs, and all the intersections. In our workshops, we try to get participants to find some aspect of their identity that might help them relate to students in their own classrooms. We believe that all educators can be intentional about inclusion and equity, and many different learners stand to benefit as instructors incorporate these ideas into their course designs and student interactions.

It is important for us to state clearly that while we invite educators to think about all forms of student diversity to improve learning for everyone, this should not minimize the historic and systemic barriers that certain groups of people have faced. The year 2020 opened many people's eyes to the racial injustices Black people in America face, and we're hopeful that the discussions, reading groups, and pledges many made to learn more will help move aspects of society and education forward. We acknowledge that not all learners begin at the same starting line because of systemic barriers, and some have more obstacles along their path. Reaching these end goals of equity requires careful attention to those who are traditionally excluded. This means that some students will need to make much larger gains than others to close these preexisting opportunity gaps.

Just as some educators don't see diversity and inclusion as having anything to do with their courses, we face the same skepticism from some students. For example, our own institution began including questions on our end-of-course student evaluations to learn how diversity and inclusion were being embraced in all undergraduate classrooms. The questions included a set of closed-ended rating scale questions as well as opportunities for open-ended remarks from students such as "How did the diversity of your classmates contribute to your learning in this course?" Many students in courses that did not address diversity issues directly responded to evaluations with statements such as:

- "It didn't, the class is too big."
- "What does math have to do with diversity?"

If we aren't direct about how diversity is a strength to be leveraged in our classroom, our students do not recognize it. Interestingly, for us and our colleagues who put inclusion at the core of their practice, students in these courses shared remarks that were characteristically different:

- "It is interesting that even in a STEM course, Dr. X makes an effort to allow students of the class to understand we are all diverse and encourage us to respect each other's viewpoints. The diversity of my classmates definitely helped me learn a lot more in this course."
- "When Dr. X polls the class on varying viewpoints, the diversity of the class definitely shows because there is a wide range of opinions. I learned about how other people see different issues, and I think that there were a lot of different ideas brought up due to the diversity of my classmates. It was interesting to be able to hear other people's perspectives."
- "Dr. X cleverly designed the course to get the most class participation and critical thinking on the individual, small-group,

and large-group level. The clever use of poll questions to enhance our learning and challenge our assumptions was a vital part of this collaboration, which I greatly appreciated. In science, people will have different ways of approaching and solving problems and engaging in this microcosm of scientific discourse was very well-suited for this course. Peer mentors facilitated this dialogue when students got 'stuck' beautifully."

We contend that so long as diversity, equity, and inclusion are relegated to only certain disciplines, offices, or individuals on campus, they will never become an ethos adopted by all. If we, as a society, value diversity, equity, and inclusion, then every member of the community should make them part of their work.

What Is the Role of Structure?

When we explored scenarios with our hypothetical students, Vanessa and Michael, we said they could benefit from more structure in classroom facilitation and course design. We'll continue to use the word structure often in this book. To some, the word may seem to imply a rigidity in approach. Instead, we suggest structure is a form of organization and a means of thinking and acting intentionally. Intentionality means we don't leave it to chance that good things happen. In a nutshell, chance won't get us closer to our goals of equity. Structure will.

Unfortunately, some instructors see structure as something basic they shouldn't have to do with students in higher education. Consider a typical question asked at our workshops: "Isn't structure just hand-holding? Shouldn't I expect my students to be able to take notes without me providing a framework?" To this we have a few responses. The first is to point out that we all need and appreciate structure even when we know how to do something. For example, think about the writing accountability groups that many scholars join. While most scholars are confident in their ability to write in their discipline, these accountability groups meet regularly and set deadlines, a structure to ensure projects move forward. Our second response to the question of "hand-holding" is to discuss who might be left behind without a particular structure. Wouldn't an outline for a lecture allow a multilingual student a better opportunity to participate? If our goal isn't weeding out students, why wouldn't we want to include structures that benefit some students greatly without disadvantaging others?

Our role as educators is to help our students learn, and not just some students. As we'll discuss throughout this book, structure plays a key role in inclusive teaching. For one, it provides the organization, scaffolding, and accountability many students may need. We cannot assume that all our students know how to succeed in our courses, or even in college. This *hidden curriculum*, a phrase often used to describe the unstated rules and norms of an educational context, means that some students know it and use it to succeed while others are in the dark about what they don't know. Additionally, incorporating structure in a course has been shown to improve student outcomes—and improve them disproportionately for those who are underrepresented in higher education, as we'll explore more in chapter 2. Thus, structure helps provide a mechanism for equity. Lastly, structure conveys intentionality in course design. When done well, it can create and foster a culture where diversity is valued and inclusion is embodied and modeled. Because structure plays such an integral role in inclusive teaching, we will be providing practical suggestions throughout the book for how to create more and better structures for inclusion. We'll help readers identify patterns and places where structure could be added in their own courses.

We like to think about inclusive teaching as an overlay or mind-set to what we might be doing already. For example, let's examine an active learning continuum, adapted from the interactive, constructive, active, and passive (ICAP) model of cognitive engagement (Chi & Wylie, 2014). Students may move along this continuum throughout class, depending on what the teacher is doing. Let's look at the model and then think about how to overlay an inclusive mind-set.

On one end of the spectrum (left side of figure 1.1), students are passive, such as when they are listening to a lecture. Students become active if they take notes while the teacher lectures. As we move along this continuum, we see students become more engaged as they construct ideas, such as when students are answering a question posed by an instructor in a pause in the lecture. Students become most engaged during interactivity, such as when they are constructing ideas collaboratively. If we envision interactivity in a classroom, we might see an instructor circulating around the room to assist pairs or groups of students as they solve problems together and the room might be quite noisy. Sudent engagement changes as an instructor makes pedagogical decisions.

How does inclusive teaching fit into this continuum? We always ask ourselves, "Who is being left behind by my pedagogical decision to do X? What can I do to add more structure to help include them?" For instance, when we need to lecture,

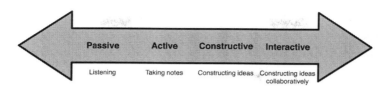

Figure 1.1. An adaptation of the Interactive, Constructive, Active, Passive (ICAP) Model of Cognitive Engagement. Adapted from Chi & Wylie, 2004.

we think about what structures we can provide to ensure that all students leave with good notes and improved note-taking skills. What can we do to help multilingual learners who can't always keep up with the pace, students with learning differences, or students who haven't had the privilege of instruction about how to take good notes? We've seen some instructors provide all the slides or notes to students, but that strategy can lead to passivity and doesn't empower students to learn to become better note takers.

How do skeletal outlines promote inclusive engagement? These outlines are designed with some level of organization but intentionally lack certain details. Students fill in the details while listening. This strategy helps students who might struggle with taking copious, organized notes, and importantly, this structure will not harm those who have mastered this skill.

Moving along the continuum, we both facilitate a lot of active learning in which students are constructing ideas, both independently and collaboratively. However, active and interactive does not necessarily equate to inclusive. In later chapters, we will discuss many practical strategies for inclusive facilitation of activities. For now, let's consider a few simple strategies as concrete examples.

As teachers, we quickly learned that when we ask a question verbally to students in class, many students miss the question or need to hear it again. Having a slide with the question clearly visible allows all students to access the question, as many times as they need. We can imagine this being very helpful to a multilingual student, as well as a student sitting next to a distracting peer.

A few years ago, we hosted a campus discussion about barriers to inclusion in a classroom. Some comments from students stayed with us long after the event. One student remarked that they felt excluded when the instructor said, "Turn to a neighbor and discuss." They noted that everyone paired up around them, often leaving the student to negotiate finding a partner or working alone. We didn't ever want one of our students to feel left out. Now consider if this student were a person of color in a primarily white institution, a female in a male-dominated topic of study, or any number of individuals who might feel excluded in different environments. We asked ourselves, "How can we bring more structure to small-group discussions and include more learners?" By assigning partners or having students count off ones and twos, we can ensure that students are not left on their own to navigate these situations. Remember, chance won't get us closer to our goals of equity. Structure will.

Why Focus on Inclusive Teaching?

"Did you know that I never raised my hand to answer a question once in college?"

Kelly shared this with Viji, after knowing her for many years. Viji replied, "Me neither." It wasn't surprising, as we had often spoken of the challenges of teaching as an introvert, but it was the first time we reflected on ourselves as introverted students in a classroom.

Kelly remembers trying to blend into the back of the class in her first college biology class in 1992, hoping not to be stereotyped in her first college academic experience. She loved the class, because the professor used skeletal outlines to accompany his chalkboard lectures. These methods allowed her to draw and think deeply as she took notes. Kelly didn't raise her hand to answer any questions the professor posed to the class, because from her perspective at the time, it didn't seem to serve any purpose to her own learning. In a not-so-comfortable, nor FERPA-approved turn of events, her professor walked over to her while handing back the first exam and made a comment about how she had gotten the highest grade in the class. He said, "Everyone should endeavor to be like her." Sinking into her seat with a flushed, red face, Kelly felt even more certain that she wouldn't be speaking up in this or any class.

Viji remembers her first women's studies course. She was excited by new ideas that allowed her to think critically about her experiences growing up in an Indian immigrant family where gender roles and expectations often clashed with Western ideals. She remembers many times when the instructor would pose a question and ask students to discuss it in small groups. As soon as a classmate began speaking (she was never first), Viji was so focused on the peer's thoughts that she couldn't construct her own. Later, as part of her graduate studies, she encountered a survey that included the statement: "I often think about what I will say before I say it." She immediately recognized that this is what kept her from being able to meaningfully contribute to a discussion—she required some time to think silently and consider what she would say. This realization helped explain why she had rarely spoken up in her classes.

In reflecting on most of our courses in college, we were both engaged, but we missed many opportunities to build on the engagement with peers and professors who did not know us. In many ways, our experiences as students, and now as instructors, shaped the way we think about the definition of the word inclusion in education. Perhaps we're trying to be the teachers we wished had engaged us when we were in college.

We've attempted to outline some of the reasons we're proponents of an inclusive teaching mind-set and associated strategies. Throughout the book, we share studies, anecdotes, and our own thoughts about the topic. Much of what we share has been offered by others as effective teaching methods, and we are collating great ideas from the perspective of inclusion and equity. It is our intent to translate these ideas into practical, actionable steps that can be employed immediately. As practitioners ourselves, we value simple tweaks we can make, particularly when much of teaching involves more laborious efforts. That's not to say some readers won't arrive at the conclusion that they need to redesign a course, but we don't think it needs to be an all-or-nothing approach. We have often reached our goals with what James M. Lang's book *Small Teaching* describes as "small but powerful modifications in our course design and teaching practices" in incremental changes (Lang, 2016b). As is the case with our students, diversity means that educators reading this book will be starting from different places. Our goal is to instigate some thoughts about how to teach inclusively and help our readers improve their teaching, no matter what their experience level. The way we reach our desired outcomes is through continual improvement with an understanding that we'll make mistakes and grow from these mistakes. As Viji likes to remind others frequently, "the first pancake is usually ugly," as she encourages educators to not give up after the first try with a new strategy.

Whether we work with educators in person or with readers of our work, we hope the outcome is that more educators are inviting a more diverse group of students into their disciplines. We all benefit from a diverse group of problem solvers in every discipline. Institutions have been investing more and more in retaining their enrolled students, especially as enrollments decrease nationally. On our own campus, we recognize the extraordinary efforts of staff who work in various student success offices such as learning centers and retention offices. We asked ourselves what role can we play as educators alongside these efforts? How can we help students realize their potential and feel included and supported in their success?

Remember, as you read this book, the authors were two quiet undergraduates who often didn't find ways to be included in the classroom conversations. We have a lot to say now, and we're excited to share some practical tips in the chapters to come. We're grateful to you for taking the time to read these ideas and committing to improving your practice of teaching.

INSTRUCTOR CHECKLIST

Adopt an inclusive mind-set:

- Ask yourself in every pedagogical decision you make: "Who might be left behind as a result of this practice?" and "How can I invite those students in?"
- Recognize that inclusive teaching practices are broader than content and discipline. Furthermore, inclusive teaching practices are effective teaching practices.
- Acknowledge that there are differences among students and that diversity is an asset to be leveraged in the classroom.
- Because our students, courses, and culture are ever-evolving, inclusive teaching is a process that will never be complete. Teaching inclusively requires our persistent attention.

Embrace structure:

- Do not assume your students know how best to approach your course. Embed resources and assignments that help make how to succeed transparent to all students.
- Consider how students will be held accountable to complete aspects of the course that are essential to success.
- Overlay structure in your active learning approaches.

CHAPTER 2

THE VALUE OF STRUCTURE

Kelly attended a workshop many years ago in which the facilitator showed a video, a parody of teaching and learning in a typical college class. In the video, the professor lectured about ballroom dancing, drawing choreographic configurations on a chalkboard all semester. The students demonstrated their boredom in as many exaggerated ways as they could. A last scene showed the students at their final exam. They were brought to a gymnasium for the first time, where they had to demonstrate proficiency dancing with a partner in order to pass the class. Students were unprepared and dismayed, to say the least.

The video left quite an impression, staying with Kelly to this day. It absurdly highlighted what we are sometimes blind to in our disciplines: that the end goals for learning need to align with the semester-long practice. In other words, whatever we want students to accomplish at the end of the course has to be practiced deliberately throughout the semester.

Let's say your goal for students is to be able to critically analyze research literature. Relying solely on watching someone else do this in a well-organized lecture is not going to get most students there. Students will need multiple opportunities to practice analyzing research studies for themselves, with feedback from an expert. Without practice for all, those with previous experience doing this kind of analysis may excel, while students without prior experience may be lost. We can imagine a professor taking credit for the students' success and blaming those who do not excel—when in fact, the professor did not have much to do with the outcomes. The inequities in skills that existed before the semester began were carried through to the end of the semester.

For practice to be effective and inclusive, it must be structured and required in your course—not optional. We're all familiar with "not optional" practice. Consider how new drivers learn to drive. Numerous safety studies over the years have led to graduated driving programs in every state. For example, in North Carolina, new drivers must now log sixty hours of distributed practice with a parent (ten of the hours at night). Once licensed, the new driver needs to continue practice under limited conditions for six months; there is a curfew and they cannot have more than one friend in the car. These laws are based on research and they protect everyone. Most people would agree that requiring sixty hours of practice for new drivers is a good idea. If new drivers don't complete the practice, the negative outcomes are serious.

There are also negative outcomes in a course if students aren't required to engage in a certain amount or kind of practice that is distributed over time. What might be the consequences? Some subsets of students won't become proficient in the concepts and skills. Other more serious outcomes are higher drop or failure rates, students leaving a discipline they were once interested in, and, in some cases, students exiting higher education altogether. In a classroom that doesn't require practice for all students, some students will have the know-how to study and practice on their own. These students may have the time and motivation to do all of the "extras" to be prepared. They may be privileged with social capital. Some students will not have the know-how. To be clear: we are not suggesting that certain students lack motivation to succeed, but rather that they may not yet understand the approaches it often takes to succeed. These could include students who are first in their families to attend college, students who come from underresourced backgrounds, students with learning differences, or perhaps students who come from different cultural backgrounds where expectations or norms about education may differ. These types of students might be the ones shouldering the majority of negative outcomes when we do not embed the know-how to succeed in our coursework.

In this book, we will advocate for the concept of high structure. This includes establishing the practice required for learning and recognizing that a rich and firm structure helps all students when minimum requirements and expectations are put in place. Putting structure in place doesn't harm students who already have the skills for practicing. But it does help level the playing field for the diverse groups of students who have not yet developed that skill. In other words, it brings some equity to educational opportunities.

Before we dive into more thoughts about setting structure and expectations, we want to clarify that this chapter is about the importance of structure in designing a course. Thus, we won't be focused on the individual curricular elements, such as assignments or assessments, as much as on how the individual pieces make the whole.

What Do We Mean by High Structure?

Let's think about a course design we would characterize as low-structure, one that leaves some at an unfair disadvantage. Dr. Slim, our hypothetical professor, wrote a syllabus with a chapter listed beside each class meeting time and a topic stated in a short phrase. The students are expected to do the reading before class and be ready for a class discussion. In class, Dr. Slim uses a mostly lecture-based approach, occasionally asking questions, and volunteers raise their hands to answer. Over the semester, students are required to demonstrate their proficiency through one analysis paper, one midterm exam, and one final exam. Dr. Slim provides some optional review sessions and guides for success.

How might students with competing demands on their time *behave* in Dr. Slim's course? Based on our years as educators, our best guess follows. Many students will not do the reading, because there is no accountability for the reading. They will decide that Dr. Slim just summarizes it in lectures anyway. Only a subset of students will participate in class, because many are not prepared (they didn't do the reading, after all) and because there is no incentive or requirement for raising their hands to participate. Most students will not review their notes until they are asked to take an exam or write a paper. Many students will produce low-quality work, because they didn't take the optional opportunities to practice and Dr. Slim's expectations were not explicitly established. While behaviors might be similar among many students, the reasons some don't do the work might be different: not knowing best practices in learning, poor time management, lack of motivation or interest, to name a few. Nonetheless, it would be easy to imagine Dr. Slim telling a colleague, "except for a few bright ones, these students are lazy and underprepared."

What could we suggest to Dr. Slim to increase course structure and include more students in the learning? As in a home-design reality show, let's conceive of a makeover to turn Dr. Slim's course into a high-structure course. In the high-structure course, Dr. Slim lists specific pages that are most relevant to the upcoming class with explicit goals for what the students should take away from the readings. Dr. Slim requires students to complete and turn in guided reading questions (GRQs) *before* class that include new vocabulary and foundational concepts. Other days, the pre-class assignments include required discussion board posts or online quizzes related to videos or readings. *During* class, Dr. Slim highlights the day's objectives and poses questions that all learners are required to answer through group discussion, individual writing, and anonymous polling (see chapter 5 for various types of ideas). Dr. Slim uses these in-class questions to ask more probing questions than the pre-class work and to debunk misconceptions in the discipline. Lastly, *after* class, Dr. Slim's students are required to synthesize short responses to essay prompts or answer exam-like questions that help them reflect on their learning of the stated objectives. Students receive feedback about whether they are meeting expectations or not in a timely fashion. Now Dr. Slim's class has incorporated elements of structure that make it clear to all students how best to succeed in the course with clear expectations, routine practice, and frequent feedback.

In Dr. Slim's high-structure course:

- the work before and after class is not optional for students.
- the level of difficulty increases as students move from pre-class work to in-class activities to post-class homework.
- students have guidelines, expectations, and opportunities for practice before they are evaluated.

How might students *behave* in Dr. Slim's high-structure course? Once again, we have a great deal of experience with student behavior in our high-structure courses. Most students will distribute their work before, during, and after class because it is required of them as part of their final grade and for social interactions in class. If they are accustomed to cramming a few times in a semester, they may complain that the course is a lot of work or something along these lines. However, high structure can lead to efficiencies for a student. Spacing out their studying each week may lead to less cramming before an exam. We've both had students come to office hours seemingly seeking our permission to *not* stay up all night like they often did before other exams because they felt like they had practiced a lot already. In fact, in a study of biology students at Eastern Michigan University in which the instructor moved from low- to high-structure design, students reported spending less time studying outside of class, even though student performance increased (Casper, Eddy, & Freeman, 2019).

In sum, the work is not optional in high-structure courses and there is required practice before, during, and after class. How do you require something of all students? We find that a few points toward a participation or homework grade, or something equally low stakes, motivates most students. Additionally, when students know there will be structured social interactions for everyone in the class (such as discussing a concept in pairs) they don't like feeling unprepared. We hope we've emphasized that the design of the assignments can easily be scaffolded to increase thinking levels and skills as a lesson progresses from before to after class. The scaffolded practice combined with continual feedback in the high-structure course equates to all students having a clearer road map or know-how for meeting expectations.

Table 2.1 The elements of a low-, moderate-, and high-structure course

	Graded preparatory assignments (example: reading quiz)	**Student in-class engagement** (examples: clicker questions, worksheets, case studies)	**Graded review assignments** (example: practice exam problems)
Low	None or <1 per week	Talk <15% of course time	None or <1 per week
Moderate	Optional*:1 per week	Talk 15–40% of course time	Optional*:1 per week
High	≥ 1 per week	Talk >40% of course time	≥ 1 per week

*Need either a preparatory or review assignment once per week, but not both
Source: Reproduced by permission from Eddy and Hogan 2014

Kelly and her collaborator defined structure in her 2014 study (Eddy & Hogan, 2014). See table 2.1 for one way to define course structure.

How Can I Prepare My Students for a High-Structure Experience?

High structure is new to many students and can be uncomfortable. Consider a student comment from a course in which the instructor requires an upload of guided reading questions and the completion of reading quizzes before highly active learning class sessions:

"I did not like the layout of this course. I do better when I am being taught material. Instead, in this class I felt like I came into class expected to already know everything. I felt like I had to teach myself more than anything. Class time only consisted of being quizzed on the material when I did not feel like I knew

it that in depth yet, as I do not learn well from just the textbook. I would much rather have class consisting of a real lecture of the material telling me what everything is."

We have found this sentiment expressed more than a few
times in our courses. Students see independent practice as
"not teaching." They see quizzing or learning from peers as
"not teaching."

In our experience, one way to dispel these myths with
students is to repeatedly remind them about how learning
works and that we created the materials that guide them
through the learning objectives. This is part of our *teaching*.
The activities in class, which promote deeper thinking in the
more difficult concepts, were also designed by us and are
about increasing student success. This is how we *teach*.
Ideally, every student would come to us knowing more about
the process of learning. Often, this is not true for many college students and is rarely recognized by educators. Unless
your institution has a required course where all students
are exposed to best practices in learning, we recommend
that you explain the reasoning behind your teaching choices
transparently and frequently in your interactions with students. We like to imagine we are running a semester-long
marketing campaign for how learning works and how we
are aligning our teaching to these best practices. We'll use
phrases like this after an active learning exercise: "I expected some of you to struggle through that activity, but I
wanted you to make mistakes to help you realize that your
understanding of that concept was not quite as deep as you
thought it was just by reading about it in our homework" or
"Look how much the whole class has improved on this concept simply by justifying your thoughts to each other. That
kind of practice helps us build connections in our brains."

These continual reminders about how we've designed the course to focus on how learning works begins to sink in for most students and become a point of appreciation.

Because many students do not have a grasp on how best to learn, they don't appreciate that deep learning is difficult and sustained work. Cognitive science reminds us: learning takes effort and needs to be distributed and varied. We see these principles incorporated in the way people learn to drive: not in one or two sessions around the same route, but over many days and weeks on many different roads. In Dr. Slim's redesigned course and in our courses, increased structure makes clear the learning cycle: practice before, during, and after class. In the end, we know incorporating requirements for best practices in understanding their learning process is going to help more students and be more inclusive.

Why not help students learn cognitive science by presenting evidence to them? For example, Viji shares with students a study from 2002 on student procrastination. Nestled deep in the article is a finding that the more distributed the work is, the less enjoyable it was for participants (Ariely & Wertenbroch, 2002). It is reasonable that people would choose to mitigate certain challenging tasks by doing them quickly, much like ripping off a bandage. However, in the case of producing high quality work, which this study was measuring, the slow and steady approach created the best results. She decided to share the study with her students to draw the parallel about their daily preparation before class. Viji acknowledges that it may not always be enjoyable, but that it is evidence for distributing learning before, during, and after class. A phrase she repeats often to help students move away from cramming knowledge that will be easily forgotten is "easy in, easy out," which is not what we want for learning. It is helpful to consider the ways you might communicate with your students that effective learning will be deliberate and structured and not without effort.

Let's be realistic. When learning requires effort, many students may articulate this as frustration in their end-of-course evaluations. These comments can dissuade an educator from implementing a high-structure experience for their students. On top of that, designing a high-structure course requires a great deal of effort by the instructor, at least initially. Educators may wonder if it is worth the effort or may be reluctant to abandon strategies they have implemented for years (such as a set of canned lectures). But while students might be put off initially by the work demanded in a high-structure course, many of our students' comments provide reasons to implement and stick with it. As the learning cycle becomes part of their routine, learners will start to feel success in a variety of ways. Here are some comments we collected from our own and colleagues' students in high-structure courses:

- "The course is well designed, with a good amount of homework to review topics and plenty of resources that are provided to get help that we need. It is apparent that the instructor cares about our success."
- "Although I was initially critical of the guided reading questions, they helped me grasp the material more than just reading on my own. I'm so glad you required them because I probably wouldn't have done all of them otherwise."
- "The course really challenged me and helped me to develop better study habits."
- "The course was organized to reduce the barriers to success: that is, course assignments were laid out clearly with many reminders, and also many ways to self–check that assignments were completed. The only burden on students was to learn the

material, not to spend time on organizing course assignments or produce our own checklists. The course was also structured to discourage procrastination, with homework and quizzes serving both to ensure students were keeping up with material and also to reinforce learning that material."

- "I wanted to personally thank you for a great class. I'm a transfer, this is my second year—and your class is by far one of the best I've taken . . . ever. Sure, I griped about the workload, but looking back on everything we've covered and completed this semester is so impressive. Your sincere desire for us to succeed is so refreshing and appreciated."

The value of structure is perhaps even more obvious to students in an online course. During the COVID-19 pandemic, as face-to-face courses abruptly transitioned to remote, students across the country expressed various sentiments that often amounted to frustration with a lack of structure. Whereas many emergency remote classes left students feeling that they were on their own with "busy work," well-designed online courses are more intentional about how students experience an organized learning environment. As Flower Darby and James M. Lang note in *Small Teaching Online: Applying Learning Science in Online Classes*, students given a series of structured video assignments build their confidence and self-efficacy steadily through the semester in a task that once seemed nerve-wracking to them (Darby & Lang, 2019). They point out that when structure is in place around course design, as well as expectations like participation, students learn what it takes to succeed.

As we have outlined here, an intentional design with high structure is vital to inclusive teaching. Whether in person, online, or both, being transparent with students about your rationale for the design and how learning works can be crucial to its success.

Is There Evidence That More Structure Is More Inclusive?

While high structure includes active learning, they are not the same thing. We have much evidence that active learning improves learning, retention, and success for more students (i.e., is more inclusive), yet not all implementations result in positive outcomes compared to lecturing (Freeman et al., 2014). Complications arise because the execution of active learning varies in effectiveness. Thus, we don't think the terms "active learning" or "flipped classroom" describe what we have been talking about when we talk about high structure. It is possible for active learning activities or a flipped classroom to have little structure (i.e., the pre-class work and post-class work is optional, and students don't have much incentive for attending and participating in class). We choose to focus on a few studies that show the benefits of active learning plus a focus on the effectiveness of structure and spacing out learning (Lang, 2016a). Many of the studies around course structure have been done in the sciences, often comparing courses that have been redesigned to incorporate more structure.

In a well-designed study, Scott Freeman and colleagues tested the hypothesis that implementing reading quizzes and/or extensive in-class active-learning activities and weekly practice exams (high structure) would reduce failure rates in a very large enrollment introductory biology course at the University of Washington, compared with lecturing and a few high-risk assessments (low structure) (Freeman, Haak, & Wenderoth, 2011). By controlling for the difficulty of exams across six semesters with the same instructor, the researchers found failure rates dropped from 18.2 to 6.3 percent after increasing structure. If one definition of inclusive is helping more people stay in a discipline, then this study surely provides evidence that high structure is inclusive.

But how does structure affect certain groups of students? Kelly and her collaborator Sarah Eddy followed up on Freeman et al. and asked this question across six semesters while Kelly was redesigning her large enrollment introductory biology course (Eddy & Hogan, 2014). She increased course structure by adding guided reading questions, required pre-class reading quizzes, and required in-class participation. On average, performance improved for all students, but Kelly and Sarah's study garnered national attention because they found a disproportionate benefit for some student groups. Gaps in performance closed for first-generation college students compared to their non-first-generation peers when more structure was added. Differences that existed between Black and white students were halved. Data collected through student surveys suggested some possible answers to why performance improved. Students were more likely to do the pre-class work when it was required instead of recommended. All students felt a greater sense of community under moderate structure. Additionally, there was an "in-class participation gap" for Black students that disappeared under the moderate structure because all students were required to have discussions with peers. Thus, while structure benefits all students, some groups of students can benefit even more.

Sometimes when discussing course redesign to emphasize additional structure, people question if it harms some students, particularly those who have been high-achieving in low-structure environments. To address this, Viji and her collaborator Quinn Moore examined the impacts of incorporating additional structure in Viji's redesigned introductory statistics course, by requiring students to watch short videos prior to class sessions (Sathy & Moore, 2020). Rather than listening to demonstrative lectures during class time, students were asked to watch them prior to class. Each class then started with a quiz to incentivize preparation. Class sessions were used to work collaboratively through problems or begin assignments. Rather than focus solely on a single measure such as an average gain or loss on achievement for students, they examined how students' scores at different points in a grade distribution were impacted. They found that the redesign amounted to a roughly similar positive result along the distribution of about four to six points. In other words, all students benefited from the additional structure regardless of where they were in the achievement distribution.

The University of Washington and the University of North Carolina represent research institutions with selectivity in their admissions. You may be wondering about the effect of course structure at institutions with higher acceptance rates and more socioeconomic diversity. A study was conducted with biology students at Eastern Michigan University, which admits almost all applicants to its undergraduate program. Nearly half of their students are from low-income backgrounds, 35 percent are transfer students, and 35 percent are from minoritized groups. Anne Casper et al. found that all students performed better under higher structure and differences between minoritized and non-minoritized groups disappeared under this structure (Casper, Eddy, & Freeman, 2019). Interestingly, the type of required assignments used at the University of North Carolina (pre-class readings and reading quizzes) did not produce similar positive outcomes when they were replicated at Eastern Michigan.

The increased performance and elimination of disparities occurred only when the required pre-class work centered around instructor-created videos, not readings. This study indicates that structure matters, but the strategies used to carry out structure may need to be tailored to the course, students, and institutional context.

Lastly, a metadata study led by Elli Theobald included data from more than 50,000 undergraduate students and reinforces the idea that active learning alone won't produce outcomes that disproportionately help underrepresented student groups (Theobald et al., 2020). They found that only when 67–100 percent of total class time was spent on active learning were disparities in performance narrowed. Specifically, they found that inequities in achievement were reduced when there was structured deliberate practice paired with a culture of inclusion. They defined deliberate practice to include focused effort toward improving performance, scaffolded exercises aimed specifically toward deficits in understanding and skills, immediate feedback, and a recurring cycle of these activities. A culture of inclusion centers on a genuine interest and care for students' success, confidence in their ability, and treating all students with dignity and respect. Theobold et al. suggest that it is not only our skill in evidence-based teaching but also our commitment to inclusive teaching that may yield the most promising results in terms of equitable learning.

What Are Some Practical Tips to Build More Structure into Course Curricular Resources?

As we discussed in chapter 1, we see inclusive teaching as a mind-set or overlay, so it is useful to consider what you are already doing with your courses and ask how to make them more inclusive. If you are new to teaching, you have the benefit of designing with inclusion in mind from the beginning. Below, we'll explore a few common strategies to increase structure in curricular materials.

Before we jump into some quick tips, it's important to note the large body of literature related to universal design in learning (UDL), a framework for providing students multiple means of engagement, representation, and action and expression (CAST, 2018). It's often easiest to introduce the concept of universal design through its roots in architectural design, implemented since the 1950s. For example, a ramp into a doorway helps someone in a wheelchair, yet it also helps someone pushing a stroller or another person rolling a cart with supplies. Thus, while stairs may be accessible to most, the extra option of a ramp ensures more people can enter the building. Thomas Tobin and Kristen T. Behling, coauthors of *Reach Everyone, Teach Everyone,* say that universal design for learning can be implemented with a "plus one" mind-set (Tobin & Behling, 2018). In Tobin's *Teaching in Higher Ed* podcast interview with Bonni Stachowiak, he explains, "think of all the interactions that you have in your course. . . . And if there is one way to have that interaction now give [students] one more way to have that interaction" (Stachowiak, 2018). For example, if the goal of a pre-class assignment is to gain some foundational content, students might be offered the option to either read an article or listen to a recording of similar material. Listening might be easier for someone who is visually impaired, but it also helps a student who must drive two hours each way to campus.

Our interpretation of using UDL in the classroom is to think about how to make the requirements in our classes accessible to as many learners as possible. But realize we said *requirements*. Coming to class prepared with knowledge is a requirement we have because that is part of the before-during-after high-structure learning cycle we discussed above. UDL allows us to reflect on how to structure aspects of our course to enable different kinds of learners but within some of the high-structure requirements we have for all students. The tips we discuss below are the ones that come up most with colleagues, and they fit into the UDL framework. (We recommend looking at the UDL framework on CAST's website, https://udlguidelines.cast.org/, as an excellent visual summary.)

Are You Assigning Readings?

Some students will feel overwhelmed and lost if a large amount of reading is assigned. Consider providing guided reading questions (GRQs) that help all students actively discern the most important takeaways from the reading and that align with assessments. To bring high structure through guided reading questions, make the readings required and not optional. Perhaps students can turn in or upload their responses to the GRQs. Perhaps students can be required to answer a few quiz questions about the reading either online or during class. Following the UDL plus one framework, can students choose one of multiple ways to demonstrate they have gained knowledge from the reading (e.g., take a quiz, post to a discussion board, or make a video reflecting on the reading)?

Are You Assigning Videos?

As with guided reading questions, a set of required questions or reflections can help a student stay focused on the video and take notes about the main points. It is not uncommon for instructors to assign videos only to find out through data analytics on a learning platform that many students did not watch it. As with readings, accountability may come in the form of quiz questions or posts to a discussion board. Embedding questions within the video can increase engagement and effectiveness as well (van der Meij & Böckmann, 2021). Another consideration with videos (assigned or shown in class) is to be sure there is closed captioning or an accessible transcript. Beyond hearing-impaired and multilingual students, many people can benefit from captions and transcripts. This is a good example of UDL.

Are You Lecturing?

Our students might also struggle with distraction in its many forms. Consider providing skeletal outlines that students can take notes on, so that they don't have to write everything down, but must stay actively engaged to fill in *parts* of the outline. For students who can't physically take notes themselves or cannot attend class on some days, a recording of the lecture would allow more students to learn. Some students who were present in class might want to watch the recordings as a way to review at their own pace. Instructors can record the class session and post it on the learning management system for all enrolled students to access.

Are You Asking Students to Engage in Activities during Class?

Determine if you have made the prompt for in-class activities clear and accessible to all. We like to put up a slide that shows the prompt in a colored box so that as the semester goes on, students immediately know that the boxed text contains their directions. While we often read the directions aloud too, the visual prompts are used by all students multiple times, as they refer back to the goals. Alternatively, prompts can be written on worksheets.

Are You Asking Students to Use an Online Discussion Forum?
With the swift transition to remote learning in 2020, many instructors, including us, realized we didn't have much experience with online teaching. Through webinars, we looked to leaders like Flower Darby, co-author *of Small Teaching Online*. Many educators were questioning her about a lack of engagement from students with online discussion forums. We were struck by some of Flower's simple suggestions for better engagement, which boiled down to two words: more structure. She suggested requiring students to have a certain number of posts or replies, being clear with students about when posts are due, and providing guidelines about the nature of the posts (e.g., whether citations are needed or not).

Are You Providing Lesson Objectives in Your Course Materials?
An objective is a short statement about what a student should be able to know and do after a lesson. In addition to course-level objectives, we recommend providing objectives for each lesson for added structure. Consider starting class with a list of objectives for the day's class and check these off as you move through class. This provides clear expectations about what is coming and what you have accomplished. These objectives can also easily be turned into study guide questions.

Are You Providing Resources That Help Students Learn?
If you are providing resources to help your students learn to write, study for an exam, or any other activity that is an integral aspect of your course, ensure that students complete it by making it a requirement. If the resource is optional, some students will know to take advantage of it or allocate the time to complete it and some students will not. As we

often like to say of resources on our learning management system: just because you post it doesn't mean they will use it. If you have designed a resource to help your students succeed, bake it into the course requirements and do not make it optional. Additional structure can be incorporated at this level. For example, you can require that a study guide is completed by making it an assignment before an upcoming exam, ensuring that everyone engages with a resource that you have designed for their learning.

These tips are not exhaustive. They are meant to help you reflect upon ways that adding structure can enhance inclusivity. We have found it most useful when educators brainstorm with each other on ways to make their curricular materials more inclusive, as there is no one right way. If done well, there will be many options for including more students.

Structure plays such a vital role in inclusive teaching that we devoted this whole chapter to the idea. Structure can facilitate inclusion and promote equity in the classroom. We find it empowering to think that we, as instructors, can help level the playing field for our students by incorporating more structure. We hope you feel the same way. Designing your courses with high structure and helping your students understand your design decisions will help them learn your course material better. When done well, this additional structure will also give students insight about who they are as learners and how they learn. We think that is an exciting opportunity: to help students become more self-aware and to build their confidence as learners. We will continue to explore an inclusive overlay in the way we structure course design, facilitation, and student interactions in the chapters that follow. In the next chapter, we will discuss how to incorporate more structure in the design of a course and syllabus.

INSTRUCTOR CHECKLIST

Create a high-structure course:

- Establish required work routines before, during, and after class sessions.
- Pre-class work such as readings or videos should include accountability for completing it. Keep the difficulty level lower as students are being introduced to the concepts.
- Have clear objectives for each class. Pose questions that all learners are required to answer in various modes. Ask questions that probe deeply or get at misconceptions.
- Establish a consistent pattern that requires post-class work such as assignments, quizzes, or discussion board posts due a certain number of days after class. Aim for timely feedback for post-class work. Align the difficulty with the level you expect of students in a high-stakes assessment.

Teach students about learning to help them buy into high structure:

- Explain to students that learning is difficult and requires effort. The effort must be routine and distributed. Perhaps share an idea about learning that students are likely to relate to, such as learning to drive.
- Frequently explain how what you are doing in your teaching aligns with how learning works.

Build more structure in course curricular resources:

- Bring structure to pre-class readings with guided reading questions and a required component to demonstrate they have completed the reading. Check that the readings are accessible to students who need accommodations.

- Bring structure to pre-class videos with guiding questions and a required component to demonstrate they have watched the video. Check that the videos are accessible to students who need accommodations.
- For lectures, provide skeletal outlines. Consider providing recordings of lectures for enrolled students.
- For in-class activities, make sure the instructions and prompts are clear, visible, and accessible to all.
- Bring more structure to online discussions with clear expectations around the number of posts and replies and guidelines for posts.
- Use daily objectives in class, checking them off as you proceed.
- If you have resources to help students learn (such as a study guide), don't assume all students will use them. Require completion by all students to ensure equitable engagement.

—

CHAPTER 3

DESIGNING YOUR COURSE AND SYLLABUS WITH AN INCLUSIVE MIND-SET

—

Remember the great debate about synchronous versus asynchronous course design during the COVID-19 pandemic? In a challenging time, we rejoiced that many of these conversations centered on empathy and equity for students. Some educators asked, "How will students without access to reliable internet be able to attend synchronous classes?" Others said, "Imagine being a student in five asynchronous classes lacking a reason to get out of bed and start coursework when you know you should." While many of the issues brought up during these conversations were not new—student populations were always diverse—many educators and administrators were new to these conversations about equitable course design and strategies.

These conversations about teaching during the pandemic pushed higher education to a new tipping point around empathy for students that we hadn't witnessed before. "Never let a crisis go to waste" was a phrase we were hearing and taking to heart. We pushed our colleagues to consider issues around access and equity and said, "Why should students have to wait until the first day of class to get a syllabus to know if the course design is right for them?" There was no pushback. A team at UNC-Chapel Hill built a tool that worked with our registration system, allowing instructors to enter useful course information before students registered for their third semester of coursework during the pandemic. Not only was there room for instructors to let students know the balance between synchronous and asynchronous teaching, but there were places to enter details about the components making up the final grade, course resources, whether there were group projects, exams, and anything else that would help a student make an informed decision using instructor-created expectations. We're hoping this tool continues to increase transparency for students as more instructors get in the habit of using it before registration each semester.

Instructors think about many elements when they are designing a course. As we dive into the design of a course, we'll consider the primary document that conveys this to students, the syllabus. From there, we'll more deeply explore a few areas represented on a syllabus, such as the learning resources, the time spent on tasks, and the grading scheme.

How Can I Align My Syllabus with My Inclusive Teaching Strategies?

A syllabus is one of the few documents that all courses share. We've seen hundreds of syllabi through various research projects and through our roles as administrators in our office of undergraduate education. Despite the myriad of resources available to help instructors write a syllabus, we're often shocked by how little some educators use the opportunity to communicate with their students. How do students get more information when they have access only to a syllabus that simply lists a few topics and dates and required statements? They ask peers and they go to sites like RateMyProfessor to see what they can glean about the instructor and how the course is set up. A minimalist syllabus may be effective, but some syllabi are minimalist in the way that says, "I don't care." Let's first explore the tone of a syllabus.

What Is the Tone of My Syllabus?

We may have constraints in terms of what we include on our syllabi, but the tone we take in writing them is largely left up to us. Compare three different syllabus statements and how they make you feel as a learner.

Statement 1: "Students shall conduct themselves in a manner that will not disrupt the learning of other students. Cell phones may not be used in class FOR ANY REASON! All personal devices must be silenced prior to the start of class."

Statement 2: "As research on learning shows, unexpected noises and movement automatically divert and capture people's attention, which means you are affecting everyone's learning experience if your cell phone, pager, laptop, etc., makes noise or is visually distracting during class. For this reason, I ask you to turn off your mobile devices and close your laptops during class."

Statement 3: "This course will require you to use your laptop and/or cell phone during class time. Research suggests that the human brain is not as excellent at multitasking as we think it is. Please be respectful of your classmates and restrict your use of digital devices to course content only. If we see that you or your peers are distracted, we will ask you to put your devices away or ask you to leave the class, and you may forfeit your ability to earn participation points that day. There will be times when you have completed your work or answered a poll question, but your peers have not. We ask that you assist your peers when appropriate or use the time to review your notes while you wait. I understand that your devices connect you to your friends and family (a wonderful thing!) but the classroom should be a place apart, however briefly (even if it seems like an eternity to you), from the outside world and distractions. You will learn more if you concentrate on the course while you are here and your classmates will thank you for not impeding their ability to learn."

The tone of the first statement is what Cornell's Center for Teaching Innovation describes as "mechanical [or] dictatorial." We sometimes see this play out in lots of "do not's" and often in LARGE CAPITAL LETTERS. This can feel like a student is being reprimanded, often before the student and instructor have met. As the historian Kevin Gannon reminds us older folks, "AVOID USING ALL-CAPS SENTENCES FOR EMPHASIS, as that is now seen as how one yells at other people on the internet" (Gannon, 2018). Also notice that the first statement is only in the third person and uses the phrase "students shall," whereas statements that are more student-centered use first-person words like, "I" and "you" and "we." Gannon has a simple suggestion in his book *Radical Hope: A Teaching Manifesto*—read the syllabus as if you were a student. He provides the structure we like to see with a thoughtful checklist he's already designed for this purpose (Gannon, 2019).

Both the second and third statements are more student-centered, a good base for thinking about an inclusive syllabus. Research suggests that warmth in a syllabus can positively influence student perceptions of the course and instructor (Harnish & Bridges, 2011). Many schools and centers for teaching and learning offer advice about tone and language, as such impressions can set the stage for a rewarding educational experience. We suggest reading a syllabus aloud or asking a peer to review it for tone. And when you see something you like in someone else's syllabus, ask to borrow it (this is what Kelly did when she saw the third statement on Viji's syllabus).

Just as educators use rubrics to assess their students, rubrics can be effective for evaluating syllabi. Consider one element of a syllabus that is often addressed: instructor availability. The information conveyed and the tone used will vary widely, but this range can be systematically assessed with a rubric. For example, Roxanne Cullen and Michael Harris published a rubric for student-centeredness, and the accessibility of the instructor is one criterion assessed. (Cullen & Harris, 2009). In table 3.1, you get a sense for how you could use Cullen and Harris's scale to quantify and classify instructor accessibility on a variety of syllabi.

When we take time to reflect on each syllabus element systematically, such as how we convey our own availability to students, designing a syllabus to be student-centered and with a supportive tone seems more manageable. As we provide more ideas throughout this chapter, you shouldn't feel you have to implement every tip or feel guilt for realizing a suggestion is too labor-intensive for you; it is the whole of what you do with your comfort level and your students in mind that matters. For example, Kelly is not as comfortable

Table 3.1   Rubric designed to measure instructor availability

1	2	3	4
Available for pre-scribed number of office hours only; discourages interaction except in class or for emergency	Available for pre-scribed number of office hours; provides phone and email but discourages contact	Available for more than prescribed number of office hours; offers phone, email, fax, home phone; encourages interaction	Available for multiple office hours, multiple means of access including phone(s), email, fax; holds open hours in locations other than office (e.g., library or union); encourages interaction

Source: Cullen and Harris 2009

giving her first-year students her personal cell phone number, but Viji does give hers for emergency purposes to junior and senior students, who have rarely used it. You may choose to implement a supportive tone differently and that is reasonable given that our courses and students vary.

Will the students notice an invitational syllabus? The importance of beginning with a student-centered syllabus is underscored by a study in which ninety students were randomly assigned to read either a teacher-centered or a student-centered syllabus and then scored the hypothetical instructor for measures around master-teacher behaviors, such as open-mindedness, preparedness, and rapport (Richmond et al., 2016). Students rated the instructor with the student-centered syllabus as possessing more master-teacher qualities and having greater rapport with students. They also remembered more of the syllabus elements than the students receiving the teacher-centered syllabus. Additional studies assigning students to similar syllabi with "friendly" or "unfriendly" tones led students to rate the instructor with friendly language to be more approachable, caring, and motivational (Waggoner Denton & Veloso, 2018).

Thus, if you've designed a wonderful course, make sure the syllabus offers students a warm invitation.

What Kinds of Statements Help Me Communicate My Commitment to Diversity, Inclusion, and Equity?

Beyond tone, we can be transparent with students about ways we show them we are building an inclusive classroom. We can add statements directed at certain groups of students with whom we have been trained or certified to work (see examples below) alongside more general diversity and inclusion statements directed at everyone.

Let's examine a specific example. An accessibility statement is something many institutions encourage or require to be on a syllabus. Students new to an institution may not know about the institution's accessibility resources. Here is a statement from our university:

> "The University of North Carolina at Chapel Hill facilitates the implementation of reasonable accommodations, including resources and services, for students with disabilities, chronic medical conditions, a temporary disability or pregnancy complications resulting in difficulties with accessing learning opportunities. All accommodations are coordinated through the Accessibility Resources and Service Office. See the ARS Website for contact information and relevant policy documents."

To this formal statement, we add notes of encouragement such as "please feel free to message me or speak with me about how I can help with accommodations." We often send an individual note early in the semester to students enrolled in ARS services to let them know we have received their request for accommodations and that we're committed to their personal success.

Have you done any certifications that demonstrate you are learning about different groups of students? We've had the opportunity to do mental health first aid and advocacy sessions for students who identify as LGBTQIA+, veterans, first-generation college students, and interpersonal violence survivors. Often, the trainings we complete provide us with a sticker to display on our office door. While these may help bring awareness to those who walk by our offices, we find it helpful to share these prominently on our syllabus, since many students won't be coming by our physical door. We often use icons, similar to the stickers on our door, as quick visuals on our syllabi.

Years ago, our own students helped us see that we needed to be more explicit with diversity and inclusion statements. Kelly was advising a student group called oSTEM (Out in STEM) that was pushing for the biology department to adopt a diversity statement that would be on all syllabi. The students and faculty worked collaboratively to create the statement before faculty adopted it.

Inclusive teaching is about wanting all students to succeed and believing they all can with the right support. We unequivocally believe this, but how would our students know if we don't directly tell them? They might assume that we, as STEM professors, believe in a "weeding out" mentality they have heard about or possibly experienced. To counteract any assumptions students might have and make our own sentiments very clear, we use the syllabus as the first place to convey our ideas about student success and belonging. You too may consider adding sentences such as these:

- "I want you to succeed and thrive in my course and at this institution. I care about you (yes, really!)."

- "Every aspect of this course is designed by me to help you successfully complete the learning objectives."
- "You have worked hard to be here; you belong here. Congratulations on your achievements, and welcome to the course. I'm excited you are here, and I hope it will be a great semester."

There are a myriad of statements and ways to demonstrate support for specific marginalized student groups. Looking through our inclusive teaching mind-set lens, it is important to remember that adding this level of structure (a statement for all students) helps the students that need to hear it, but it won't harm the students who don't need these affirmations to succeed. In table 3.2, we include a few more ideas and a sample statement that can be adapted to use more first-person language. If you find one you like midsemester, keep a copy of it handy and make a note to add it to your syllabus for next time. Be careful to review the text periodically, as language and culture can change, and your statements may become outdated.

Does My Syllabus Highlight My Commitment to Content about and Created by a Diverse Group of People?

In his book, *Radical Hope: A Teaching Manifesto,* Kevin Gannon describes a moment when he realizes he's been using books almost exclusively authored by white, male, senior scholars (Gannon, 2020). And yet in his teaching, he openly told his students to consider the importance of diverse perspectives, especially from marginalized groups. The next time he taught the course he used only literature from female scholars. He didn't make an announcement calling this out, and he wasn't sure the students even noticed. At the end of the

Table 3.2　Example statements for a syllabus

Type of statement	Example statements (all statements would have specific contact information linked as well)
Inclusion	It is my intent that students from all diverse backgrounds and perspectives be well-served by this course, that students' learning needs be addressed both in and out of class, and that the diversity that students bring to this class be viewed as a resource, strength and benefit. It is my intent to present materials and activities that are respectful of diversity: gender, sexual orientation, disability, age, socioeconomic status, ethnicity, race, culture, perspective, and other background characteristics. Your suggestions about how to improve the value of diversity in this course are encouraged and appreciated. Please let me know ways to improve the effectiveness of the course for you personally or for other students or student groups. In addition, in scheduling exams, I have attempted to avoid conflicts with major religious holidays. If, however, I have inadvertently scheduled an exam or major deadline that creates a conflict with your religious observances, please let me know as soon as possible so that we can make other arrangements. (University of Iowa College of Education 2016)
Success statement	You have worked hard to be here; you belong here. Congratulations on your achievements, and welcome to the course. I'm excited you are here, and I hope it will be a great semester for all. (Sathy and Hogan 2020)
Accommodations based upon sexual assault	The University is committed to offering reasonable academic accommodations to students who are victims of sexual assault. Students are eligible for accommodation regardless of whether they seek criminal or disciplinary action. If a student comes to me to discuss or disclose an instance of sexual assault, sex discrimination, sexual harassment, dating violence, domestic violence or stalking, or if I otherwise observe or become aware of such an allegation, I will keep the information as private as I can, but as a faculty member of Washington University, I am required to immediately report it to my Department Chair or Dean or directly to the University's Title IX Coordinator. (Washington University Center for Teaching and Learning n.d.)
Multilingual statement	Brown welcomes students from around the country and the world, and their unique perspectives enrich our learning community. To support students whose primary language is not English, services are available on campus including language workshops and individual appointments. For more information, contact . . . (Brown University The Harriet W. Sheridan Center for Teaching and Learning n.d.)

Table 3.2   Example statements for a syllabus

Type of statement	Example statements (all statements would have specific contact information linked as well)
Reporting bias	Penn State takes great pride to foster a diverse and inclusive environment for students, faculty, and staff. Acts of intolerance, discrimination, or harassment due to age, ancestry, color, disability, gender, gender identity, national origin, race, religious belief, sexual orientation, or veteran status are not tolerated and can be reported through Educational Equity via the Report Bias webpage. (Penn State University Faculty Senate, n.d.)
Mental health	As a student you may experience a range of issues that can cause barriers to learning, such as strained relationships, increased anxiety, alcohol/drug problems, feeling down, difficulty concentrating and/or lack of motivation. These mental health concerns or stressful events may lead to diminished academic performance and may reduce your ability to participate in daily activities. University of Minnesota services are available to assist you. You can learn more about the broad range of confidential mental health services available on campus via the Student Mental Health Website. (University of Minnesota University Policy Library n.d.)
Basic needs security statement	Any student who has difficulty affording groceries or accessing sufficient food to eat every day, or who lacks a safe and stable place to live, and believes this may affect their performance in the course, is urged to contact the Dean of Students for support. Furthermore, please notify the professor if you are comfortable in doing so. This will enable her to provide any resources that she may possess. (Goldrick-Rab 2017)
Trigger warnings	I've done my best to identify any texts with potentially triggering content. I've included tags for: violence, racism, misogyny, and self-harm. If you have concerns about encountering anything specific in the course material that I have not already tagged and would like me to provide warnings, please come see me or send me an email. I will do my best to flag any requested triggers for you in advance. (University of Michigan n.d.)
Resource costs	I acknowledge that textbooks and course materials are an expense for students, and I've made efforts to reduce costs by . . . [list costs if any, if copies of materials are on reserve for free at the library, if lower cost alternatives are available, if sharing is possible]. (Sathy and Hogan 2020)

(continued)

Table 3.2 Example statements for a syllabus

Type of statement	Example statements (all statements would have specific contact information linked as well)
Respect/civility	Your instructional team affirms our commitment to the following, and encourage you to as well: • respect the dignity and essential worth of all individuals • promote a culture of respect throughout the university community • respect the privacy, property, and freedom of others • reject bigotry, discrimination, violence, or intimidation of any kind • practice personal and academic integrity and expect it from others • promote the diversity of opinions, ideas, and backgrounds that is the lifeblood of the university. (Mt. Holyoke College n.d.)
Feedback statement	I welcome your feedback so that I can make this experience better for you and all students. This link will take you to an anonymous survey, available all semester, that will allow you to give me feedback at any point in the semester. (Sathy and Hogan 2020)

semester, every student gave unsolicited comments in their course evaluations about the positive value of the readings for the semester. Gannon continued to diversify his reading lists, being much more intentional about his selections, and he found the course was far better for these changes.

While Gannon did not disclose the identities of the authors on the reading list, you don't need to shy away from this. We think it's a great idea to highlight content and authors that align with your goals. There are numerous, various ways to do this, including some call-out in the syllabus. For example, you might create your own internal logo that symbolizes a spotlight on diversity or add a "syllabus quiz" question that draws students' awareness to variety of authors. As our colleague Jean DeSaix likes to paraphrase from the Bible and remind us, if you've done the good work "don't hide your light under a bushel basket." In other words, be transparent with students about your commitment to diversity and inclusion.

Our syllabus is one of the first introductions our students get to the design of our course. Consistent with our theme of structure, we advocate that reading the syllabus be required so that it is not left to chance that only some students know how valuable it can be. We know many instructors who link a quiz or assignment to the reading of the syllabus.

We often spend weeks and months designing other aspects of the course and curriculum beyond the syllabus. These other aspects, such as the cost of resources, what and how much content is covered, and the grading schemes are just some areas that require consideration around diversity, equity, and inclusion. Let's dive into the course resources and content first.

What Should You Consider in Choosing Your Course Resources and Content?

If Students Are Paying for Resources, Are They Getting the Value?
At our university years ago, the student government began a campaign for affordable textbooks and other course-related resources. Instructors were asked to sign a pledge that includes asking educators to recognize the overall costs students face, research affordable options, and communicate with students in a timely manner about costs. We were curious about the pledge and wanted to better understand their goals, so we met with a few of the students for a conversation. The students expressed a simple goal: they wanted instructors to think more about student costs in their course planning. Students felt particularly vexed by instructors who required the purchase of one or more resources that were not used in the course. They expressed discontent with the perceived misalignment between instructor expectations and the reality of how they actually taught. For example,

they said, if a professor summarized the readings in lectures, then why not list the book as optional rather than required? They also added that there were instructors who ran out of time in the semester and didn't use a particular book that the students had already purchased. The summary of our conversation with these students likely represents how many students around the country feel:

- Students know that educational materials may require expense, but they want to know that educators are researching open-source versus copyrighted content to reach their learning goals.
- If a student is required to purchase materials, they want low costs and want materials to be heavily utilized to get their money's worth.

How do students get value from a resource? The answer to this question aligns with our discussion of structure in course design. In an example of a low-structure course, an instructor assigns readings, but then lectures on the content students were asked to read. The readings become optional; only some students do the reading, creating inequities in who gets additional practice. Before Viji incorporated higher structure, very few any students would complete the assigned readings because there was very little incentive to do so. In a high-structure course, all students are required to do the readings and associated practice before class. When Viji redesigned her course, she began each class with a short quiz, explicitly showing students that she expected all students to come prepared. Students see the value of any purchase if the instructor expects all students have utilized it and then launches into deeper learning activities and collaboration during and after class.

Do You Emphasize Content Too Much?

A common start to many posts on Twitter is "I don't know who needs to hear this right now, but . . ." Tweets like this often provide permission to do something different. So we don't know who needs to hear this right now, but your job as an educator is not to cover all the content, it is to ensure that all students learn.

As STEM instructors who teach introductory courses, we often find ourselves in this predicament of what needs to be covered for the next course in the curriculum versus what students can reasonably learn in one semester to remember and use in the next course. Sure, we can turn on a firehose of content, but then the instructors in the next course (sometimes ourselves) will lament that the students don't remember even the most fundamental concepts. The University of North Texas Teaching Commons framed a solution nicely: "Instead of covering content though, what if instructors uncovered content? Uncovering content leads towards an entirely different approach to course design, learning, and teaching. Uncovering content assists learners in developing a base of knowledge necessary to accomplish course outcomes" (UNT Teaching Commons, n.d.). Uncovering content often includes helping a learner see how a field is organized or how knowledge is acquired and assessed. A review by Christina Petersen et al. echoes a similar message in which the authors advise instructors "to view content as a collection of concepts, competencies, and facts to be deliberately selected rather than a list of topics to be covered" (Petersen et al., 2020).

How do many educators design a course? One way we have gained insight to answer this question is with our work with the Summer Institutes on Scientific Teaching on our campus and others. From the many instructors we have worked with, we've learned that course design is often a solitary practice that either follows a list of topics represented as chapters in textbook or is a version of some other instructor's course. In the Summer Institute, we teach educators to design a course deliberately, from a set of outcomes that they and others in the discipline think are most crucial. We know firsthand that it can be difficult to move away from tradition. Asking educators to start with the outcomes, such as what students need to know and be able to do, is something that is new to many. This kind of course design—beginning with the outcomes, determining acceptable evidence of the learning, and then designing learning activities to reach these goals—is known as backward design (Roth, 2007). In past Summer Institutes, we've put educators from similar disciplines together and asked them to list outcomes they think are most important in an introductory course in their field. The result is that only some of the outcomes they design are content-related. Many of the outcomes are competencies, such as being able to analyze data or design a controlled experiment. This exercise creates a dissonance for some, especially the more experienced instructors, as they think about what they value versus the course(s) they have designed in the past. In first learning about backward design, many educators become convinced that they need to be more deliberate in designing the courses. After this reflection, instructors often realize that they need to make room for other important ideas beyond content, but it can be a struggle getting there.

We have worked with faculty colleagues who have determined that they are ready to more fully incorporate essential competencies to their teaching, such as evaluating evidence. However, they feel their course is unique and has too much essential content. What often follows next is that if they cut content from their lecture, students won't learn it. They believe that if students don't *hear* content aloud in a lecture from them, it is not being *taught*. As we, and numerous research studies see it, the problem is that that students don't remember something just because a professor said it. By using class time for reciting content only, an educator loses the opportunity to use inclusive and active learning methods that bring deeper practice to all students (we'll discuss these methods further in chapter 5). By narrowly focusing on one teaching strategy, an educator negates all the ways students can learn and practice independently on their own before and after class by reading, answering questions, watching videos, having online discussions and so much more. Revaluating the content coverage is an essential part of the journey an instructor makes when moving to a more student-centered course.

We've seen how one well-known study helps instructors who are on this journey create a more student-centered course by lecturing less. This specific study comes from a physics education team, led by Carl Wieman, in which two sections of an introductory physics course were compared for one week's worth of content. One section was taught by an experienced tenured professor in a standard lecture. The other section was led by an inexperienced postdoctoral fellow and graduate student who facilitated learning through problem solving and group discussion activities. The practice the students received in the active section affected students' learning dramatically: students did twice as well on a twelve-question multiple choice concept test (Deslauriers, Schelew, & Wieman, 2011). This study and many others demonstrate that relying on lectures alone is not best for learning, and that all students can improve if the instructor employs a variety of strategies. This improvement is the crux of inclusive teaching: moving the needle for all students, not just some. Data like these open the conversation for possibilities to teach the same content differently or to spend class time practicing skills and competencies in addition to lecturing.

Just as instructors are held accountable for our students moving from one course to another in a curriculum, we are collectively responsible for graduating students who have important skills and competencies that will make them effective in whatever comes next. For example, we sometimes hear that employers are disappointed that graduates are not skilled in oral or written communication, something that every general education curriculum likely emphasizes. If the general education curriculum is deficient in these soft skills, some students may be seen as less prepared because they didn't have the ability to participate in experiences such as unpaid internships, travel, and networking. How does every instructor in every discipline take a piece of that responsibility to level the playing field for all students if they are primarily focused on lecturing a lot of content?

Let's look at a hypothetical instructor, Dr. Dynamic. She believes an important outcome of her course is that students learn how to set up a solid argument. She is a brilliant lecturer and she teaches them how to do this by modeling excellent arguments in her lectures. In her course, students practice building arguments of their own by writing two papers, for which they get little feedback during the writing process. Dr. Dynamic believes she is teaching this skill, but this kind of course structure will continue to benefit the students who come in with writing know-how already. If Dr. Dynamic wants to teach all students to set up a good argument, she can't expect them to build an effective argument mainly by watching an expert. Similarly, nobody learns to swim by watching a skilled swimmer. Ideally, Dr. Dynamic would give up some class lecture time to incorporate small activities for students to practice breaking down and evaluating various arguments. Students would additionally benefit from activities in which they outline arguments and receive feedback from peers and the instructor. In sum, they need deliberate practice structured for this competency. And, no doubt, while practicing building arguments, Dr. Dynamic's students will work with facts, dates, and big ideas, while deeply learning content at the same time.

There is no right balance to competencies and concepts in one course, since each course sits within a larger, shared curriculum. We've found it useful to reflect on our own intentions by trying to quantify the amount of course time students get practicing disciplinary competencies. This helps us see if we are reaching our stated values. In a first-year writing course, students spend a large percentage of their time learning skills around communication. In contrast, an introductory survey to a discipline may devote little time to practicing communicating like a professional in that discipline. It may feel difficult to add time for competencies in an introductory course, but it all comes back to the intentional design of a course and a curriculum. With purposeful planning, we can balance competencies and concepts.

How Do We Focus on Competencies? A Case Study

Keep in mind that courses focused on a single competency, and not content, ensures that graduates get these important skills in a large dose, in addition to being scattered throughout courses in a curriculum. For example, most institutions require a first-year writing course because they recognize this is a valuable experience for all students. We thought a lot about this kind of requirement as we helped design a new general education curriculum for our own university. As a research-intensive institution, our campus highly values the outcomes gained from conducting research. Studies have shown the benefits of this kind of experience, yet we also highlight the inequities in who gets to have these experiences (Eagan et al., 2013). Reflecting on our ideas of a structured, inclusive course, we helped argue that a structured, inclusive curriculum would require all students have a research experience, and we would provide the opportunities to ensure access for all (Hogan & Sathy, 2019). To achieve this goal, our committee would rely on a set of courses across disciplines in which a large percentage of each course focused on the research competency outcomes.

We want to share our own experiences working with research competencies to highlight some rewards when content is not the main focus of a course. Helping to lead, assess, and teach within our university-wide course-based undergraduate research experience (CURE) program has given us a unique view. A CURE is a course in which the whole class is engaged in a relevant research question that is novel to both the student and the instructor and relevant to the community (Auchincloss et al., 2014). The community can be a scientific community or something more public, and students are encouraged to report their findings through academic publications and posters, community reports, or other avenues. For example, our colleagues in biology developed a course called Seafood Forensics, in which students sampled fish and used DNA-based techniques to determine if it was labeled accurately or fraudulently (Gin et al., 2018). A colleague in American Studies had students use archives and interviews to research how past lynchings in the American South affected families (Spurr, 2019). Students in these courses learned plenty of content, whether in genetics or American history, and they learned it deeply enough to be able to produce new knowledge/content that mattered to them (Korzik et al., 2019). Many of the barriers that prevented some student groups from getting involved in research were overcome by having research courses that simply required enrollment. CUREs have been shown to be an inclusive way to welcome a diverse student group into a discipline, especially when part of introductory courses (Bangera & Brownell, 2014; Sathy et al., 2020; Penner, Sathy, & Hogan, 2021). Aside from the knowledge created, rewards come in the form of opening doors to research for all students. For example, many students in our program, including Viji's, volunteered to continue writing a publication long after the semester ended. Some decided to take another CURE course and others had new confidence and skills to approach a professor to do mentored research. Some students even changed their career choices because of a single course that focused heavily on a transformative competency-based experience.

Opening doors to our discipline is a major goal we have as instructors, and we strongly believe that the questions around too much content are a big part of whether students feel welcome or overwhelmed. A simple question we often ask ourselves to help deliberately select or justify cutting content is: "Why would students care about this?" We don't mean the super-interested, driven majors in our program, but the still-deciding or non-major students in our course. Would this content get them excited enough to want to do more in our discipline? Reporting on a three-year national Integrative Learning Project (ILP) sponsored by AAC&U and the Carnegie Foundation for the Advancement of Teaching, Huber et al. ask, "Where and when are students encouraged to make links among their academic, personal, and community lives?" (Huber et al., 2007). While all disciplines need to strive to be student-centered and include curricula that students can use in their everyday lives, this is highly prominent dilemma in STEM. Numerous reports have detailed the crisis of STEM and have provided road maps for how to improve curricula (National Academies of Sciences, Engineering, and Medicine, 2016). When we consider the disproportionate number of minoritized groups leaving STEM because of a lack of interest, we begin to see how important it is to make our disciplines relevant if we expect to diversify our fields (Seymour & Hunter, 2019). As we cut down and edit our content to our most important and relevant ideas (and feel sad removing something that we personally enjoy), we remind ourselves that being inclusive is a mind-set that requires intentionality.

Have I Chosen Content That Reflects the Diversity of People?
As we highlighted with Kevin Gannon earlier in the chapter, many educators are now paying attention to assigning readings authored by a diverse group of scholars. A movement to decolonize the syllabus aims to move away from white writers as the dominant voices in a course and ensure that voices from Black, Indigenous, and people of color are dominant. Yvette DeChavez writes in the *Los Angeles Times* on why she decolonized her syllabus based on her experiences as a young, Latinx student: "*These voices were interesting, sure, but they were so different from mine. I wanted to read something that reflected my experiences a little more, stories about what it felt like to live between two cultures at all times, stories about feeling overwhelmed by a society that tells you you'll never be as pretty as the blond-haired, blue-eyed girls*" (DeChavez, 2018). Thus, DeChavez and others stress that when we teach

content from mainly white men, we may implicitly imply that only their voices matter.

In STEM, we find a similar lack of diversity in who is visible as the authority and expert. Traditionally, textbooks and lectures focus on foundational experiments and research by white men. How do we reimagine courses to show LGBTQIA+ individuals, women, Indigenous people, and people of color as role models and creators of knowledge in STEM too? We need to be intentional about incorporating good research by diverse people who have changed and continue to change science. Some educators do this by inviting guest scientists to class or they might interview someone via videoconference. Others ensure they have good representation by using videos of traditionally underrepresented individuals delivering content (through TED Talks and such). Might we start each day by highlighting a scientist? For example, Kelly made sure to start one of her biology classes discussing the work of a Black woman named Kizzmekia Corbett (an alumna of UNC), whose research was a major contribution to the development of the earliest COVID-19 vaccines. In this vein, Schinske et al. describe Scientist Spotlight assignments that replace textbook readings so that students read about the background of diverse scientists related to content being learned (Schinske et al., 2016). STEM educators can find guest speakers and researchers to highlight through various sources such as online interviews, TED Talks, Project Biodiversify.org, databases like "1,000 Inspiring Black Scientists in America" and "500 Queer Scientists," and connecting with people through hashtags like #BlackinSTEM and #womeninSTEM on Twitter.

In some disciplines, having diverse content that represents different people and viewpoints is a deliberate goal of the course. Many arts and humanities courses fall into this category. Yet in our own fields in STEM, we find that incorporating diverse content has been slower to develop. In fact, the Howard Hughes Medical Institute (HHMI) echoes this in a call for their Inclusive Excellence Grant (ie3), "In the last several years, significant attention has been given to the way we teach (e.g., active learning, "flipped" class-rooms, peer-led team learning). However, we haven't paid as much attention to what we teach and revising the content of the introductory experience lags far behind improvements in pedagogy" ("Inclusive Excellence," n.d.).

Educators who don't teach subjects that are inherently about diversity and inclusion often feel unsure about what to include in their discipline related to these issues. This sentiment was expressed in a workshop we did at our university, in which we anonymously asked faculty to express one of the challenges they faced in supporting diverse students. One quote represents the uncertainty most of us feel: "I'm unsure I'm presenting material that reflects and represents the diversity of the class." We've both found online materials, conversations with colleagues, and open discussions with our students have helped us incorporate more diverse content. For example, Kelly, a biologist, included readings about intersex differences in humans and consulted with staff at the LGBTQIA+ center to make sure the reading was appropriate and culturally sensitive beyond the biological content. Viji, a statistician, included an assignment in which students collected and analyzed data about how a diverse group of students felt disrespected by professors and peers. The assignment opened many personal conversations beyond statistics. It is useful to continually reflect on ways you can gradually add more content (or update outdated content) related to diversity of identity and experiences in your own course.

Conversely, some content in STEM disciplines can work against our goals in this area. At an event with minoritized students in STEM, one discussion group became passionately involved in a conversation about the overuse of the same example they were seeing in many biology and chemistry classes—sickle cell anemia. They expressed frustration that the only time Black people were discussed in STEM classes was in this negative context. This is a notable example of how tradition and textbooks weigh us down with examples we might not think to replace. It doesn't have to be this way. We need to think beyond the traditional examples and value our students as partners who can help us with these challenges, if we allow them to participate in finding solutions.

Representing the diversity of people in our courses is a task that is never finished. With our inclusive mind-set, we should continually ask ourselves if our course represents the diversity of content creators (authors, artists, and researchers) and contains substantial content about human difference.

How Much Time Are Students Spending on Your Course Tasks?

When Kelly was first thinking about redesigning her course from a traditional lecture-only format, she paired up with a colleague from her Center for Teaching and Learning who helped her put together a survey to examine student perceptions about the course before she made changes (a "control" semester). The responses could be compared with students in future semesters in a redesigned course. The survey asked simple questions that Kelly had never asked her students before. For example, the survey asked students how much time they spent working on Biology 101 outside of class. The average was one to three hours per week for her three-credit course. (As with most universities, she had been told students could expect spending six to nine hours per week on a three-credit hour class.) She now had a starting point for when she began requiring students to practice via weekly assignments. Not surprising to her, the average time spent outside of class increased in the next semester.

The time a student spends on a course and how they distribute their time can be important factors in fine-tuning an inclusive course. A dense reading or lengthy assignment may penalize students who are balancing many responsibilities outside of class or might require more time for some students than others for various reasons (if they are learning in a second language, for example, or have learning differences that make reading a struggle). We suggest getting an accurate estimate of the amount of time students are spending on your course work. Knowing the amount of time students are spending on tasks allows instructors to be transparent about their expectations, which lets students plan accordingly. Alternatively, it's possible an instructor finds out the students are spending too much time on some tasks and begins trimming to the most important.

Technology has helped us answer some questions related to timing. For example, many learning platforms provide learning analytic reports for individual and class averages, including the amount of time spent on certain assignments or watching videos. An app developed by Betsy Barre and colleagues automatically estimates course workload based on instructor inputs about assignments (Barre, Brown, & Esarey, n.d.). We're likely to see more and more technology that helps us get a handle on data like these.

Another approach is to poll students routinely, to get a better sense about the week-to-week differences. For example, Viji incorporates a question on an assignment that asks the students to report the amount of time it took to complete that specific assignment. In midterm feedback, she includes a poll asking students to estimate the number of hours spent outside class completing the routine components of the course. Often, the data show that most students are spending the expected amount of time. By asking and debriefing with students at the midway point she demonstrates she cares and affirms that learning effectively takes time and effort.

Why would you want to know about the amount of time students spend on your course, whether through technology or polling? First, students are diverse, and knowing who the outliers are can help an educator reach out individually to a student. Second, knowing the average time spent per task allows an instructor to make this information transparent on the syllabus or at the beginning of specific assignments. Students of different backgrounds and responsibilities will be able to better plan for the necessary work and balance this with other responsibilities. Thus, conveying time-on-task information provides two important components of inclusive teaching: structure and intentionality.

Can Grading Schemes Be More Inclusive?

When we write a syllabus, we inevitably find ourselves quickly determining how we will calculate final grades in the course. How will we weight the different components? There are so many different grading schemes out there. As individual instructors, we may not have the freedom to make changes to this aspect of our courses. For example, if we teach a departmentally coordinated course, have a co-instructor, are part of a multisection course, or have mandated institutional policies, we may not be able to dictate how grading is determined. Nonetheless, we think it's worth reflecting on and advocating for grading schemes that help more learners make it to the finish line successfully.

Let's follow a real student's educational path to explore this concept. When Viji started college, she was a premedical student. She took a year of general chemistry and biology. In her sophomore year, she did poorly on her first organic chemistry exam. She considered dropping the course because there were only two more exams making up her whole grade. She ultimately finished, but this course caused her to leave her premedical track.

Many courses have grading schemes like these—two or three high-stakes assessments making up most or all of the grade. In fact, some disciplines and programs have this high-stakes grading scheme as the culture of what they do. Consider the language of a prominent law school: "To a great degree, a student's final grade in many of the courses offered at NYU School of Law is dependent upon the grade received on the final examination. As a result, adequate preparation for the examination cannot be recommended too highly" (NYU School of Law, n.d.). The thought of this very high-stakes exam scares even us! What if something tragic was going on in our lives that day? What if we had a migraine or terrible cramps that day? Besides the myriad of reasons why different students might not be able to demonstrate their fullest knowledge and skills in one performance, the underlying message seems to be focused on choosing, culling, or weeding out students.

Creating more assessments that each count less toward the final grade is one way to move away from the single or few high-stakes assessments we described above. Besides multiple exams and papers with lower weight, many instructors will put some of the grade toward other low-stakes assessments and components that are not based on accuracy, but rather on completion or participation. Other instructors may throw out exams altogether and move toward many small assignments or quizzes. From a measurement perspective (an area of expertise for Viji), there are other good reasons to shift away from fewer high-stakes grades to more frequent lower-stakes grades. Increasing the number of assessments helps provide a more consistent reflection of a student's learning and allows both a student and the instructor to identify an anomalous grade.

Besides simply dispersing the weight of grades into smaller chunks for everyone, what if Viji's chemistry grades were more personalized to her growth? For example, maybe her first grade could be dropped, or her first exam could have been weighted less since her final exam showed improvement. Intentionally considering varied grading schemes help us avoid losing talented, diverse students after one bad grade. Let's explore more of these ideas that help students see mistakes as normal, without needing to drop the course or change their major because of one poor performance.

How Can You Embed a Growth Mindset into a Grading Scheme?
We have advocated for structuring the learning cycle of before-during-after for each class and the curricular materials to support deliberate practice. Deliberate practice implicitly tells a student, "keep trying, you'll get good at this." But where in our grading schemes do we provide parallel messages like "mistakes are part of learning and not only are they OK in this course, they are expected"? These sentiments align with a growth mind-set view first proposed

by Carol Dweck: abilities can be developed with hard work and practice. Opposed to this view is a fixed mind-set, which views intellectual ability as innate (Dweck, 2006). Whether an instructor has a growth or fixed mind-set about their students' learning seems to have big consequences for final grades. Elizabeth Canning et al. studied 600 STEM courses and found that in courses taught by more fixed mind-set faculty, the racial disparities in achievement were twice as large as those in courses taught by faculty with more of a growth mind-set (Canning et al., 2019). Even among the many instructors we know who have a growth mind-set and encourage it with their students, few have intentionally baked it into their grading policies.

If many educators accept that mistake-making is a part of learning, then why do so many students, as we described above with Viji, feel like they have no options after doing poorly on one exam in one course? Why do so many alter their future goals because of one exam? If Viji was allowed to drop her lowest grade, she might have had a different outlook on this course. Grading schemes with a simple tweak like this provide hope for improvement and ultimate success. Viji's negative experience as a student led her to experiment with grading schemes that incorporate a growth mind-set. Below are some examples that help build mistake-making into the grading scheme:

- Allow a score on a cumulative final exam to replace a previous exam, enabling a student to demonstrate growth.
- Weight assessments early in the semester less heavily than assessments later in the semester to help students learn from mistakes.
- Drop the lowest grade or quiz, designating some quizzes available for retaking, and giving points back after a student

makes corrections to an exam to encourage students to reflect on their responses and motivate them to aim for proficiency of the material.

- Use flex points in which a student has to get only enough points to gain full credit. For example, some percentage of the available points (say twenty-five to thirty points out of forty) can still be considered 100 percent.

No matter what strategy is used, it is worth reflecting upon how you show students it is OK to make mistakes via your grading scheme. One bad day or one misstep need not derail a student's plans or communicate that they do not belong in your discipline.

Are You Choosing a Grading Scheme Consistent with Inclusion?

Many quantitative and qualitative studies in STEM have shown us that competition between peers is one reason that women and minoritized students feel they do not belong in or leave STEM disciplines (Hughes, Hurtado, & Eagan, 2014; Palmer et al., 2011; Shapiro & Sax, 2011; Seymour & Hewitt, 1997). One way competition is communicated is through grades, when there are a limited number of As to be earned. This is known as grading on a bell curve or norm-based grading. In this practice, an instructor says something like, "only the top 5 percent of students will receive an A in this course."

When Kelly first began teaching in 2004, with little professional development under her belt, she reached out to a senior professor who was also teaching very large science courses with hundreds of students. She's saddened now when she thinks about the tips she was given. Many of these tips induced competition among students and led to high rates of attrition. The grading advice she received was to produce a bell-shaped curve for each exam, using the mean and standard deviation. The result was a limited number of As and an equal number of Fs.

While Kelly eliminated norm-based grading early in her career, we know this strategy is still employed across the country. In a student newspaper from Johns Hopkins, student Sam Mollin made a plea to administrators in 2018 to abolish this kind of grading, for the toxic competition it spawns and the toll it takes on student well-being. "It doesn't matter if you successfully learned 95 percent of the material if 50 percent of your class successfully learned 96 percent," Mollin wrote. "Rather than earning the A you deserve on a test, a bell curve could downgrade you to a C. In a scenario like this, what incentive is there to cooperate?" (Mollin, 2018). We don't know how prevalent this kind of grading is, but we hope students across the country will continue to call it out.

Norm-based grading is antithetical to an inclusive classroom. Consider the way a think-pair-share technique creates a positive classroom environment, improves learning, and pushes students to collaborate with one another. This sense of community and collaborative learning is what allows all students, especially students who are traditionally underrepresented in our disciplines, to feel included and thrive. Yet what would be the point of promoting this in-class collaboration and community if the corresponding syllabus indicates a fixed number of As? The grading scheme sends a message in conflict with inclusive in-class activities.

"Moving away from curving sets the expectation that all students have the opportunity to achieve the highest possible grade" say Jeffrey Schinske and Kimberly Tanner in their excellent review article, "Teaching More by Grading Less (or Differently)" (Schinske & Tanner, 2014). How do they and other scholars suggest we do this? We can compare students against standards of proficiency in a field, instead of against each other. This grading practice is known as criterion-referenced grading (Turnbull, 2009). Moving toward a reference point of proficiency means that it is possible for a large number of students to earn As and reinforces the value of collaborative practices in an inclusive classroom. Viji jokingly tells her class that they should help one another conquer the material because she will retire when 100 percent of the class earns an A. Remarks like this reinforce the ideal that all students can achieve their highest goals.

We both recall the impact of learning about backward design when we were given some of our first teaching development opportunities (Roth, 2007). The idea of identifying desired outcomes for learning, determining acceptable evidence of the learning, and then designing the learning activities to reach these goals was so logical and yet eye-opening to us. It is the concept Kelly wished the senior professor had taught her, instead of the bell-curve tip. We realized that if all students became proficient in the concepts and competencies in our fields, then all students would receive an A. Did this ever happen? Not yet—but it is a goal. If you employ criterion-based grading, inevitably some colleagues will warn you that this philosophy will lead to grade inflation. We combat this criticism by showing them the student work that demonstrate evidence of the levels of proficiency. We also try to remind ourselves and colleagues that our role is to help all students learn, not selectively weed them out.

Once we learned about criterion-based grading, we got to work backward-designing all of our courses and we've continued ever since. The work is never done, though. We continue to modify our stated objectives and goals each semester. Admittedly, getting the right level of difficulty and aligning this to the right practice in class can be a challenge, even for educators who have been teaching in their discipline a long time. One resource that helped Kelly with her practice was to use a set of shared learning concepts and competencies developed for biology, called Vision and Change (American Association for the Advancement of Science, 2011). Perhaps your discipline has such guidelines. You can also tap into the expertise of experienced instructors who teach a similar course. You might ask them for their course objectives and an aligned final assessment. We've found that these educator-mentors are not always at our own institutions. Social media and professional conferences have been effective ways for us to find our people.

In this chapter, we've explored ways to intentionally design your course, including concepts around syllabus statements and choosing (or losing) content. We now turn our attention to launching an inclusive course, which begins with intentional welcoming messages and first day activities.

INSTRUCTOR CHECKLIST

Syllabus:

- Check the overall tone of your syllabus and aim for a supportive and warm tone.
- Read the syllabus as if you were a student and use student-centered language that is invitational.
- Avoid capitals for emphasis.
- Use first-person statements in your syllabus ("I," "you,"

and "we"), rather than third-person statements such as "students shall."

- Present an inclusion statement along with incorporating your inclusive practices in different aspects of course activities.
- Include specific statements about accessibility, affordability, and student success.
- List trainings you have done that relate to specific underrepresented groups.
- Highlight content and authors that relate to your commitment to diversity and inclusion.
- Ask a colleague to read over your syllabus to check for the above.
- Review your syllabus text periodically to keep it current.

Content/resources:

- Research the costs of the materials you will use in your course. Be sure that if you ask students to pay for resources, they will be heavily utilized.
- If resources are truly optional, and not required, be explicit with students.
- Research and compare open source versus copyrighted content.
- Consider your role to be less about content delivery and more about helping students learn concepts and competencies that relate to their interests, everyday lives, and the curriculum.
- No matter what your discipline, include content that relates to human diversity and be sure your content is culturally up-to-date. Value students as partners to identify problematic content or to find new content.

- Diversify who is an authority figure in your discipline by diversifying the author list, people shown in videos, and creators of knowledge in your discipline.

Time spent on course tasks:

- Determine how much time students are spending on tasks.
- When planning your course, examine how much time is required outside class and aim for a reasonable set of hours or those prescribed by your institution.
- Communicate time expectations outside class to students early in the course.
- Think about ways you can assess how much time will be spent outside the class time to complete course work and make adjustments as needed.

Grading schemes:

- Include many low-stakes assessments and move away from one or two high-stakes assessments that make up the whole or majority of the course grade.
- Embed a growth mind-set into the grading scheme. Some ideas include dropping the lowest grade, weighting earlier assessments less than those later in the semester, allowing exam corrections, replacing a semester exam with the cumulative final exam score, and allowing a less than perfect score to count as full credit.
- Use a criterion-referenced grading system in which students are graded based on proficiency of concepts and competencies. Use a backward design approach to state each learning outcome and the evidence that would allow you to see if a student has met that outcome.

CHAPTER 4

LAUNCHING YOUR COURSE

As children of the 1980s, we both grew up with the familiar shampoo commercial where one person is mocking the other for having dandruff on their shoulders. The interaction always ended with a smirk and the line "you never get a second chance to make a first impression." The same is true for professors and students, whether in face-to-face classes or online courses. First impressions are important. We enjoy talking to each other and colleagues about how we can make good first impressions. We admit that even as adult women, we still check in on the morning of our first days to confer about outfits (even though we don't want comments about our appearances!).

But what if all that planning for a first impression boiled down to only thirty seconds or less? One study was conducted with students in a focus group who were shown three ten-second silent clips of college instructors they did not know. Students rated them on a variety of characteristics, including "supportive" and "warm" (Ambady & Rosenthal, 1993). These two characteristics, and several others, corroborated the student evaluations of the instructors' teaching from actual students who interacted with the instructor for an entire semester. Other studies of nonverbal and verbal brief first impressions have also reinforced the idea that the first impressions we make are often lasting (Babad, Avni-Babad, & Rosenthal, 2004; Tom, Tong, & Hesse, 2010). Bottom line, if you want to show your students you are going to be the kind of professor that supports all students, know they will be judging you immediately.

Face-to-face impressions are something we all plan for, but what about the impressions we make with the first emails and the way our learning management system is set up? The list goes on with ways we make impressions on our students before we meet, and all of them deserve consideration through the lens of inclusivity.

How Can I Communicate an Inclusive Welcome before the Semester Begins?

The beginning of the semester is the time to convey important course logistics to your students. It is also a time for everyone to begin getting to know one another and to start building community. The community includes you and the students, and it may also include graduate teaching assistants, undergraduate learning assistants, and co-instructors. When considering inclusive teaching, are there small tweaks you might want to make to your messaging? Have you capitalized on the attention and excitement students have at the beginning of a semester to collect information about them? The beginning of the semester is the ideal time to set the stage for inclusive practices in your course.

We always send a welcome email announcement via our university's learning management system. Sometimes this message goes out weeks before the course begins, when we wish to convey information about course materials; sometimes it is just a few days before the course begins, when we are ready to share the syllabus and course website. Assuming you have already made a thoughtful, inclusive syllabus that you want students to read, the welcome email is truly the first impression you will make. Spend a few minutes writing and editing the message to make sure it invites all students to the course, builds rapport, and conveys any important tasks you would like them to accomplish (for example, read the syllabus, take a survey, create technology accounts). Keeping it short with links to more information puts the warm welcome front and center. You might consider sending a personalized email to each student, which can be efficiently done with a mail merge function or through your learning management system.

Beyond course logistics, the welcome messages can begin to build educator-student relationships. Help students get to know you by including a bit of personal information, possibly with a link to more details or a video. Consider a short reflection about how you felt as a student before a new semester started. A note like this reminds them that you were once in their shoes. Alternatively, you can include a photo of yourself with something you did in the past year, or you with a pet, or a picture of you in college to which they might relate. This kind of talk about yourself and your experiences is called self-disclosure. Research studies show that self-disclosure has many positive student perception outcomes, such as increased interest in the course and an increased likelihood of engaging with teachers outside the classroom (Cayanus, 2004). Lowering the barrier for a student to form a relationship with you and benefit from your experience may be as simple as talking to the whole class about the latest television series you are binge-watching. Keep in mind that individuals not belonging to dominant social groups or identities in academia (for example, in the US: white, male, cis-gendered) may have to think more carefully about how much and what to share. We know from research about bias in student evaluations that what is seen as welcoming from one instructor can be seen as unprofessional from another—different standards are unfair but real (Owen, 2019). No matter how you decide to accomplish it, do think about how you can use your welcome message to build your relationship with all your students.

The weeks and days leading up to the semester can be a good time to gather more information about your students collectively and individually, some of which you might want to summarize on the first day. For example, at our institution, we have access to a bit of information before we meet our students (name, photo, major, minor, class). Other institutions provide more information. As a new instructor, Kelly used these data to learn that most of the students in her introductory biology course were not biology majors, and most were first-year students. This allowed her to do a quick hand-raising activity with students on the first day to debunk the notion that all the other students were more qualified because they were biology majors with more experience. In a pre-course survey, Viji asks students to rate how likely they were to take a statistics course if it were not required. Then, on the first day of class, she presents these data to the students as a way of sharing that data can tell a story. The story? Nearly all are in the course against their will and they have more in common than they think. Collecting data about students helps you begin building your relationship with them and, if shared, can help begin building a peer community.

What information about students do you not have from campus systems that would help you to better form relationships? A short survey can help you get this information before the semester begins or on the first day. Below are a few of the questions we have asked in our initial surveys:

- What is one skill that you have that makes you unique from many other people?
- What part of the state, country, or globe are you from?
- What do you think you will learn in this class?
- What would make the course material interesting or useful to you?
- Could you share anything about any classes you have been a part of where the instructor did some things that you thought worked well (such as anything that made the course more interesting or personal)?
- It is important to me that all members of the class feel supported, respected, and included. What does your vision of inclusivity look like in a course/classroom setting? If it helps, you can provide examples of what inclusion does NOT look like.

Besides pre-course surveys, an alternative way to gather information from students is to ask them to post their written or video responses in a structured introduction within the course management system. This more public approach allows both you and the students to get to know one another and begin building a community.

One more feature to pay attention to in setting the stage for a warm welcome is your course site. You can reinforce the idea that your course is structured to help students succeed by paying attention to the online organization and welcome you provide. Some students may log into the course management system before they read any messages from you. We like to make sure the course management page has a welcoming statement or image (Viji posts an image of a welcome mat on the front page) as well as a message.

There is one group of students who run the risk of feeling particularly excluded at the start of the term: students who are not yet registered for your course. Depending on the registration procedures on your campus, you may have students who do not gain access to the learning management system or your emails until they are officially registered. This may leave students who are waitlisted for a variety of reasons (for example, the course may be full, or there may be financial roadblocks) feeling excluded from access to vital information. Consider creating a simple web page or shared document accessible to all and post the welcome information along with any resources you ask students to access. Not only do these seemingly small gestures help unregistered students, but they convey to the rest of the class that you care about the success of all students, including those hoping to enroll in the course.

Posting information for unregistered students was one way we streamlined communications that helped us not get cranky when we received the same email questions over and over. Feeling cranky before a semester begins is counter to the welcoming tone we hope to convey. Over the years, we streamlined more logistics to benefit both us and our students. We often build a community before the semester begins through an online discussion forum in which every student can see the questions and answers. Allowing students to post anonymously (and letting them know this) allows students who don't know "how to college" to ask questions without feeling like they are being judged by the whole class. Some questions might be directed to us, such as "my financial aid doesn't begin immediately, when do we need the book by?" or to peers, "I'm a transfer student living off-campus, does anyone know the closest bus stop to our building?" After teaching a course many times, we learned the common questions and can amend our syllabi to be as clear as possible. We also often direct students to a Frequently Asked Questions website. These kinds of ideas saved us from repeating ourselves and helped us stay fresh, patient, and approachable for the first day of any semester. Let's now turn our focus to the first day.

How Can I Utilize the First Day of Class?

Imagine yourself as a first-year student in your first semester trying to figure out where your history class is located. You walk into a room that you think is correct, and immediately feel reassured because there is a slide at the front of the room that says, "Welcome to History 222." Phew! Now you don't have to ask a classmate or the professor if you are in the right location. As you settle into class, you see someone moving from one group of students to another, casually chatting with students. You surmise it is the professor and they seem nice. They are laughing and occasionally shaking hands with students. You immediately relax. This isn't so intimidating after all.

This professor intentionally used the time before class to set the tone, which would have especially benefited students with anxiety, who are introverted, and countless other characteristics. A welcome message identifying the class calms students who might be reticent to check in with others. Greeting students one-on-one shows someone who sees students as people. Even if the instructor doesn't greet all the students, many others are noticing.

Once class is ready to begin, it is time for introductions and setting expectations about your shared goals and activities for the semester. Let's dive into each of these by collating ideas about setting the stage for inclusive teaching on the first day.

What Should I Consider as We Introduce Ourselves to Each Other?

Students at most universities have internal social media sites to which they often post memes and random thoughts. We have learned much about student culture by lurking on these sites. One meme that caught our attention made us chuckle. It said "me every single day of syllabus week. . . . I'd rather take a razor scooter to the ankle than stand up and tell the class a little bit about myself" (Patterson, 2019). It was relatable to 222 other students immediately, too. It caused us to reflect upon the student experience in the first week of classes.

Do a majority of professors ask the same thing on the first day, such as "Please stand up and say your name, major, and something unique about yourself"? In our classes of hundreds of students, this is a no-go. Even in a class of thirty students, this kind of activity is time-consuming and is not the most effective way to begin building community. Apparently, it also causes students to wish physical harm to their ankles! There is a myriad of reasons why some students would not feel comfortable with this facilitation technique, something we'll explore more in chapter 5. As we reflect on the meme, we wonder, are students lamenting the repetition and predictability of saying one thing about themselves? Or do students dread vocally sharing something personal with the entire class? Since we are lurkers on this social media site, and plan to continue to be, we didn't interact with the post's author to find out.

Before brainstorming ways for students to introduce themselves to you and their classmates, we suggest that you consider introducing yourself first. Model some of the behaviors you would like them to use.

We have come to believe it is critical to share personal, fun facts about ourselves on the first day. With introverted tendencies, we find this kind of sharing doesn't always come naturally. We have found a structure that works well: we show a few photos of our younger selves and briefly share a story or two about our professional career paths and personal lives. As we take students through this lighthearted autobiography, we tell them what attracted us to our disciplines and current roles at our university. For example, Viji helps students see that her path included a bit of math anxiety, something many of the students in her course strongly feel, and how she not only got over the anxiety but came to love data. To help students see us as approachable, we also include anecdotes about ourselves, our likes and dislikes, and true/false quizzes about which characteristics they think describe us. Telling students the current show you are binge-watching might seem frivolous or unimportant, but one student articulated clearly why this matters more than we might know. This student later told Kelly, "Seeing that you watch *Grey's Anatomy* shows me that you are a normal person. And if you are a normal person with a PhD, then maybe a normal person like me can be a PhD or a physician." What is also noteworthy about this one story is that this student was a Latinx male, yet Kelly, not a male or Latinx, became relatable to him. Fun facts are more than just fun—the personal information shared on the first day may be more impactful to students than most educators realize.

What else matters to students with first-day introductions? We learned much during a session we facilitated called "Carolina Conversations: Inclusive Classrooms" with students, faculty, administrators, and staff. We asked the students to individually and anonymously fill in a notecard that said, "I wish my professors knew that I don't feel included when _____." The cards were a treasure trove of information that we refer to consistently. Related to first-day introductions, two types of student quotes now guide our introductions: "When pronouns are not asked and respected" and "When they say my name wrong." Let's explore these two basic parts of identity a bit more.

As for pronouns, we begin modeling how to share pronouns on the first day. For example, we simply say something like, "Welcome. I'm Dr. Hogan, your biology professor for the semester, and I use the pronouns she, her, and hers." Students who are part of the LGBTQIA+ community immediately notice this gesture (and sometimes thank us after class for it). Modeling demonstrates how simple it can be. Many students have never introduced themselves this way. Likewise, we model displaying it in relevant places such as an email signature and with our names in an online meeting rooms. As we were learning the value of sharing pronouns, we incorrectly assumed it would be most inclusive to ask each student to state their pronouns when they introduced themselves to each other. However, students again helped us understand why our assumption was wrong. Students kindly informed us that not everyone is at a stage where they are ready to choose a pronoun or state it publicly. Assimilating this new understanding, we learned to invite students to share their pronouns, but we never make it a requirement in any form (spoken or written). In general, this is a good principle that applies to many areas of identity. You can offer, model, and provide a safe setting, but you need not require it.

When it comes to names, we use the lens of inclusivity on both student and professor names. Should students address you by your first name? If you have a prefix such as "Dr.," should they use this and your last name? Students can't know your preferences and they often haven't been given guidelines with respect to naming their educators. Consider the effect it would have on your own biases if you were normally called "Dr. Hogan" but a student came up and called you "Mrs. Hogan." Would you make assumptions about that student, compared to others? You can see how the structure for naming is important to both you and your students. Perhaps your name is often mispronounced. Do you have a shortened version you use? One of us, Viji Sathy, owns one of those names that is often mispronounced. Throughout childhood she came to accept the fact that it would always be mispronounced. She didn't start thinking about correcting people until her college roommate asked her why her parents say her name differently than everyone else. Her roommate encouraged her to teach others how to say her name correctly. Now, when she introduces herself to her students or anyone, she teaches others how to say it. She also links an audio file to her email signature and on her syllabi and website. The audio allows people to hear her say it as many times as they need. By modeling this behavior, Viji encourages students to make their own name audio files and provide phonetic spellings. Thus, to be more inclusive, we shouldn't leave getting names right to chance; we can intentionally structure ways to invite people to share this information.

Why is name pronunciation so important? Not saying a student's name correctly can be perceived as a racial microaggression, and as researchers Rita Kohli and Daniel Solórzano describe with K-12 students, these repeated daily insults can make a student feel invisible, othered, and inferior (Kohli and Solórzano, 2012). What is often dismissed as one instructor's simple mistake is a hurtful act that has been repeated over and over in the student's life with the impact of saying "you do not belong." Actor Uzo Aduba (full name Uzoamaka Aduba) underscores this feeling of otherness when she recounts a story from childhood when she asked her mother if she could simply change her name to Zoe. Her mother said, "If they can learn to say Tchaikovsky and Michelangelo and Dostoyevsky, they can learn to say Uzoamaka" (Raisa, 2019). We don't need to have names that are uncommon in our particular geographic area to normalize students teaching us and peers how to say their name correctly. Sacharitha Bowers gives us a succinct rule if you don't know how to pronounce a name: "Do not guess, do not stare and say 'oh boy' or any number of such nonsense phrases, do not ask if [the person] has a nickname. Ask how to pronounce, listen when they tell you, repeat until you get it right" (Bowers, 2019).

Earlier, we explained how students at the Carolina Conversations event helped us learn when they felt excluded in a course or classroom. During this event, we also asked them about a specific time they felt included in a classroom. Many students commented about how a professor took the time to learn their name. If you are like us, you start to get overwhelmed on the first day about being able to remember each student's name, how to pronounce it, and which pronoun(s) they use. We give ourselves and you permission to not memorize every student's pronoun and name. Simply showing that you are trying is recognized and appreciated by most students, and your effort can start on the first day. Here are two tips to help you use and learn names:

- Ask students to write names on card tents if your classroom has tables or on folded paper that hangs down from individual desks. You can also invite (not require) them to add their pronoun and phonetic spelling of their name.
- Ask students to fill out a small notecard with their name and invite them to add pronouns and name pronunciations. You might ask them to also include other information about themselves such as major and fun facts so you can learn more personal details without every person needing to stand up to say it aloud.

Below are a few tips that we have used or collated from the educational hive mind of teachers and students regarding names and pronouns that apply on the first day and as the semester progresses.

- Using a student's name avoids the need for pronouns. For example, you can use a phrase such as, "Yes, your great comment builds on Chris's answer."
- If you do not know students' pronouns, use a more generic term. For example, we should not make statements such as "Yes, your great comment builds on *her* previous answer" but rather "Yes, your great comment builds on your *classmate's* answer."
- If your students will sit in the same seats every day, build a seating map with names of students.
- Use a photo roster of your class to learn as many names as you can. Choose a few every day. Use these names during class, even on the first day, and students will assume you know more names than you do!

Kelly did an observation of a colleague toward the end of one semester. The instructor wasn't using names when she called upon students in a class of about twenty-five students. Kelly asked the colleague if she knew the student names. They then had a conversation about the value of using names for inclusivity. The colleague later emailed her:

> "I want to thank you for our conversation about using students' names in class. When I thought about it after talking with you, I realized that there were really only about 3 students who I wasn't sure of, and so I confirmed them and started calling everyone by name after that. This semester I'm working much harder to call them by their names as soon as possible. I realized after talking with you that it was my own shyness that was keeping me from calling them by name."

This interaction reminds us all that sometimes what holds us back is ourselves. Recognizing this allows us to make small yet meaningful tweaks and changes to our interactions with students.

How Can I Align My Course Goals to My Introductory Activities?

We generally advocate using most of the time in the first class session to build relationships, create a safe environment, and convey a few broad, relatable ideas about the content. All too often, instructors focus on the content of their syllabi, when students can learn this on their own. We hear what you are thinking—"they won't read the important parts if I don't tell it to them." Providing a short overview and highlighting some of the key pieces that you want to emphasize is a good compromise without reading each aspect aloud. Best practices in learning suggest they will learn more from us asking them what is on our syllabus rather than telling them. Consider spending five to seven minutes outlining key points and then asking students to engage with the syllabus through an activity. Here are some examples to encourage more asking and less telling:

- Incorporate a syllabus quiz or a "scavenger hunt" either as a team-building activity in class or as an assignment administered through the course management site. This latter approach doubles nicely with an orientation to navigating your course site.
- Ask students to review the syllabus in small groups and respond to a set of questions such as "find one topic that you are all interested in learning about and tell me why." If your course involves a lot of small-group discussion, this could be a good opportunity to start as you mean to go by incorporating a small-group activity related to the syllabus.
- Offer an open discussion forum for students to pose and answer questions for all to see. This approach has the added benefit of being available throughout the term and encourages engagement beyond the first day of class.

Remember that students are often being given similar information in multiple courses, and we can be fairly certain they are not assimilating as much information as we think when we only tell it to them. Instead, give them the tools to make it stick and permission to refer back to the syllabus repeatedly.

As with any good class session, we recommend you write down your goals for the class and then plan activities that help you reach that goal. Below are three high-level goals that we think anyone might want to achieve on the first day of an inclusive class:

1. Begin developing the student-instructor and student-student relationships.
2. Set the stage for an environment in which it feels safe to make mistakes.
3. Have students find personal/societal relevance in your topic.

A first-day activity could meet one or all of these goals at the same time. Below are a few ideas from educators that we see aligning with these goals. These activities also begin to show students the pedagogical techniques you will use, such as think-pair-share.

Ahna Skop, a biologist, uses an activity based on a small questionnaire she developed (Landhuis, 2019). The types of questions are: Where are you from? What are your hobbies? What's your favorite local restaurant? Students complete this alone by writing answers (think time). Then they have to find someone else in the room to discuss their answers with (pair time). Students then introduce the other person to the class (share time). Skop takes notes during this time about each student. To conclude the activity, Skop reveals her answers to the questions. This activity aligns with the first goal. As a reminder, when students are introducing themselves, we should include an opportunity for them to provide their pronoun, nickname, and name pronunciation. If the questionnaire includes a question such as "what is one thing that was difficult to learn but you didn't give up on?" this could allow the instructor to include the second goal. Similarly, a question such as "how do you think this course relates to your life?" would align with the third goal.

We both carry out an activity that aligns with the second goal by allowing students to contribute to a class contract for the professor and the students in the class. We often list the first ideas, to give students a sense of the kind of ideas they may synthesize. For example, we often say, "The instructor(s) won't randomly call on anyone unless all students have had a chance to confer with classmates and can then represent what the group is thinking." We ask students to submit some ideas of their own on paper or via poll technology (think time). Next, we ask them to introduce themselves to students around them and decide on two or three ideas to later share with the class (pair time). To help structure the discussion and sharing, we predetermine the "reporter" of the group by setting some characteristic, such as "the person with the most vowels in their name" or "the person who was born farthest away." Lastly, we randomly call on a few students and ask the reporter in their group to share the group's ideas (share time) as we write them down.

Robin Roberson, a psychologist, uses pre-class readings and writing prompts throughout the semester to help students perceive "that something is interesting and worth knowing" (Roberson, 2013). This idea aligns with the third goal and is easily adapted for a first-day or first-week activity. You might print or project a jargon-free paragraph related to content in your course and ask students to silently read it. Next, give students a prompt: "How does content in this paragraph relate to your life or an issue in society you care deeply about?" You can have students form small groups and choose a few groups to share what they were discussing.

Envision yourself executing first-day activities that align with your goals. Congratulations. But did the students understand why you did what you did? Did you explicitly state the goals to them? Students sometimes have a *feeling* of inclusion, but don't fully appreciate that you intentionally designed your class session around inclusion. Here are two simple tips for being more transparent. First, post your goals (such as our goals one through three) for students at the start and end of the first class. Second, include the diversity/ inclusion statement from your syllabus in your slide deck and read the statement. Although we don't advocate reading many parts of your syllabus to them, underscoring your commitment to inclusion in the classroom is worth it.

We both feel a teacher's high after our first-class session and are thrilled when students articulate feelings of inclusion and enthusiasm for the semester. Below are a few quotes from Viji's students after the first day. You can collect these feel-good notes for yourself too by either asking students for a short, anonymous reflection before they walk out the door or with a follow-up message asking for a reflection.

Ways students found the activities more interesting than a usual first day:

- "Interesting day! Nice to get to know our neighbors (especially in a large class setting), also good to know my professor a little bit."
- "This was definitely one of the better first days I've had here and this was my 3rd year here. Normally first days are really boring and predictable. . . . This was not."

Comments about their perceptions of the instructor:

- "You've made it clear you're here to help. We'll work hard, but it will be supported. No need to be scared!"
- "I like how up front you are about everything. I feel expectations have been set and I know what I need to do! I'm excited for the semester."

Their thoughts about the discipline:

- "Math is NOT my thing at ALL. But after today's class, I don't feel quite as anxious about it and I feel confident I will have plenty of help."
- "I'm still very apprehensive, but realizing that almost every-one else is, as well, was helpful. I'm nervous, but optimistic."

What Can I Do to Wrap Up My First Week?

After you come down from your first-day teacher's high, it's time to keep up your commitment to inclusion. In closing the first day or week of class, you might want to send a thank-you email to your class, including some reflections from the first day and your enthusiasm for moving forward with a tal-ented, diverse group of students. We also recommend jotting down some notes to yourself about what worked and didn't work as planned. Personal reflection is a big part of growth for an educator, which we'll explore more in chapter 7. As educators, we'll likely have many more first days, so a quick time investment to make notes can pay off again and again. We've both found a first-day formula that works for us, so we continually repeat it, making small tweaks as needed to foster connection.

Your commitment to inclusion doesn't stop after the first week. Be sure to plan your next lessons with as much intentionality as you did the first day. Keep self-disclosing personal information about yourself in class and routine email messages. In our next chapter, we'll dig into inclusive facilitation of activities you may be using all semester. For example, we included think-pair-share in sample first-day activities in this chapter. We'll also discuss many more ideas for facilitation such as keeping time, managing small-group and whole-class discussion, polling, and more.

INSTRUCTOR CHECKLIST

Before the first day:

- Send a welcome message, including some details that help students get to know you.
- Open a discussion forum to build community and answer all questions in one place.
- Collect data you have about your students and consider sending a survey to gain more personalized information about each one.
- Make important information accessible to students not yet registered through an open link.

First day/s:

- If possible, arrive early enough to meet and mingle with students before class begins.
- Be sure the course name and your name are visible for students unsure if they have found the correct location.
- Model your introduction first and provide the name students should call you, how to pronounce it, and your pronouns.
- Ask students to fill out name cards or tents they will bring each day and invite them to add pronouns and name pronunciations.
- Use self-disclosure as a strategy to lower barriers for students to form a relationship with you. Share personal information about your life, such as when you were a student, show photos, tell students your likes and dislikes.
- Plan and show students your goals for the first days that align with inclusivity. Perhaps read the diversity

statement to them as an example of your commitment to inclusive teaching practices.
- Execute first-day activities that align with your goals and introduce pedagogical techniques that you plan to use throughout the semester.
- Assess student perceptions about their first day and how well you accomplished your goals.

After the first day/s:

- Send a message of thanks.
- Reflect on what worked and what didn't for future first days.
- Keep planning lessons intentionally and communicating routinely throughout the semester.

CHAPTER 5

CLASSROOM ENVIRONMENT AND INTERACTIONS

Let's begin this chapter with a few scenarios. Have you witnessed any of the following at a meeting?

- At a meeting to discuss a new policy, an opening presentation goes so long that there is time for only a few questions and not much discussion.
- One individual at a meeting hasn't spoken. To draw them out, the meeting leader calls on them to ask them to weigh in. The quiet individual looks caught off-guard.
- The meeting leader asks everyone to go around and make brief introductions. Most people keep it short by stating their names or connection to the project. One individual gets into the weeds about a specific issue they are having. After this person finishes, the remaining introductions are rushed and the schedule is thrown off.
- A discussion becomes heated and ideas are offered quickly by a few people dominating the conversation. After the meeting, others state that they were frustrated that they didn't have

time to process their own ideas and ways to jump into the conversation.

If you marked one or more, you have been a participant in a noninclusive environment, which now makes you the ideal candidate to cultivate an inclusive environment in situations where *you* are the facilitator. Whether in your classroom or at a meeting you are managing, an inclusive mind-set and collection of facilitation skills can be transferred to any environment. Feeling empowered as a facilitator allows you to be bold. In 2018, Kelly took her skills to her first jury duty assignment. She volunteered to be foreperson for a trial dealing with a serious crime. Her facilitation skills transferred well to a diverse group of people dealing with differing opinions and serious consequences. In these situations, it is obvious that incorporating structure helps. Kelly brought structure to the juror discussions by asking them to stop the discussion for a few minutes so everyone had time to write their thoughts on a piece of paper. She took some quick anonymous polls of everyone in the group to see how far away they were from consensus on certain details. Once you have a mind-set around structure, we bet you will see that all kinds of environments can be improved, from summer swim meets to school orientations, panel discussions, and more.

In this chapter, we will present ideas from students about what makes them feel included in a classroom. We'll then discuss facilitation strategies to improve inclusivity.

At times, inclusion is hard to pinpoint, but the floodgates open when students are prompted to think about a time when they felt excluded. Years ago, when we facilitated a campus-wide conversation on classroom inclusion, students vividly articulated what inclusion and exclusion looked like for them. Not surprisingly, many comments were focused on face-to-face time with an instructor and peers. Students completed this sentence anonymously, "I feel excluded in a classroom when . . ."

- "Faculty let certain students hijack or dominate class discussions."
- "Participation grades are only given to those who speak to the class OR when my grade depends on speaking out in class. This limits my ability to sometimes do well and also makes me feel like I do not belong or am somehow doing something wrong by being shy or introverted."
- "The professor says to talk to a neighbor, but the neighbor has other friends and I am left isolated."
- "All the professor does is talk. It is often the case where the professor only talks and goes through the lecture slides. This makes me feel like the 'learning' aspect is not important."
- "I am picked out in front of the class and don't always have the answer."
- "Another student insults me personally and the professor doesn't do anything and ignores it."
- "The professor singled me out, related to my Blackness."

A common statement from instructors is that they see higher education serving a purpose to push students out of their comfort zones. We don't disagree, but after years of collecting personal student experiences, we see that many instructors likely need better training in classroom facilitation. Effective teaching does push students out of their comfort zones and with structured facilitation, it will do so in a way that makes students feel safe and respected enough to participate.

Most educators can convince themselves of the power of good facilitation when they examine feedback from their students, whether positive or negative. When students have experienced good facilitation, they make comments such as the ones we've heard from students in our courses:

- "I loved hearing different perspectives and getting to try out practice problems on our own, then in groups, and then as a class."
- "I learned to listen to other perspectives and be open-minded in working through other people's understandings to see things differently to come to the correct answer. It also gave me practice to explain my own understanding."
- "I would also like to show appreciation for your commitment to diversity, equity, and inclusion both inside and outside of the classroom. With a class this large, it was remarkable to see how dedicated you are to ensuring that we are all taken care of and comfortable in a learning environment."

We may be our own worst obstacle in accomplishing our facilitation goals. It is common for educators preparing to teach to think, "What will I cover today?" We sympathize with getting bogged down in content coverage because we both teach introductory-level survey courses. After many years of reflection, we've concluded that if we don't put careful thought into facilitating classroom interactions, we risk losing valuable opportunities for all students to learn more deeply. Furthermore, we might inadvertently leave some students behind if we mismanage these interactions and our carefully crafted content would be lost amid stifling exclusion. In practice, this translates to two sets of notes that work in parallel as we lesson-plan: content and facilitation. We often go through a class session in our heads with these two aspects in mind, picturing students in time and space, as though we are choreographers.

It's important to consider that although the guiding principles of good facilitation are the same, the context will influence how these principles may be implemented and evolve. For example, after many years of teaching the same large statistics courses, Viji was given the opportunity to design a new course for a small group of students. It allowed her to think about an inclusive environment from the start, as opposed to continually retrofitting the design of an established course. The smaller class size meant that she could consider what kind of classroom would be ideally suited to carry out the course objectives, instead of assuming that they would meet in a lecture hall with fixed seats. Like all effective educators, we are continually examining our approaches and aiming to improve inclusion. The work is never complete because we're always moving to meet our changing students' needs. We keep a growth mind-set as we alter, evaluate, and alter, again and again.

Pedagogical strategies in higher education have not changed dramatically since medieval universities instituted lecturing to their students. And it wasn't until more recent history that the student body in higher education became more diverse, due to overturning some racist and sexist exclusionary policies of the past. Who belongs in college, how the physical space is designed, the disciplinary perspectives, and how educators and students are supposed to teach and learn have all been shaped by centuries of systemic barriers to participation. If you were to make a list of students who might not feel comfortable in higher education, who would they be? You would probably come up with a list similar to this: students who are underrepresented either at the institution or in a discipline, students who are first in their families to go to college, students who are introverts, minoritized students, those who experience imposter phenomenon, students holding a minority view on an issue, students with learning differences, those with physical disabilities, individuals who identify as LGBTQIA+, international students, and many others. While the list seems overwhelming, we always feel empowered when we reflect on how a few tools help most of our students feel more confident and comfortable. As our classrooms become more diverse, so should our educational strategies.

In this chapter, we discuss the facilitation tools we value most. Before we discuss the tools, let's explore questions that we can ask ourselves as facilitators in the classroom, independent of content and discipline.

How Can You Be an Inclusive Facilitator?

Let's start with the definition of the word facilitate: "to make easier; help bring about." To help bring something about, a facilitator needs to know what that something is and help make it happen. In a classroom, these are the learning objectives. If the facilitator holds the end goals in mind, they will plan how to meet these objectives. This brings us to the first task of a facilitator: planning.

Do You Have a Plan?
When you plan a lesson, there are many things to consider beyond objectives. For example, what evidence do you need to show you've been successful in meeting your objectives? What does the physical space look like? How can you help students form groups in this space? Do you require preparatory materials that would help everyone engage? What

specific prompts or instructions will you use to elicit a productive session? Are there various ways students can participate beyond raising their hands to speak? How will you let them know? How much time should you give to each activity?

Remember the checklist at the beginning of this chapter about meetings? The first scenario was, "At a meeting to discuss a new policy, an opening presentation goes so long that there is time for only a few questions and not much discussion." A facilitator must plan and practice to avoid these kinds of situations in meetings and classrooms.

Do You Have Rules to Help Others Stick to the Plan?

Next, we find it very helpful to think about rules of engagement or ways in which interactions will be managed between instructors and students and between students. Many instructors co-create these with students early in a semester. Once constructed, everyone is asked to stick to these guidelines. To save time and model the idea, we start the class or groups off with some example statements, such as "don't interrupt a speaker" and ask the students to add to the list.

Sometimes the group comes up with a statement that needs to be better defined or operationalized. The suggestion "be respectful" from students might need to be made more specific and transparent by calling out behaviors that are not respectful and then further defining the agreement. Along these lines, Viji asks her students to exemplify professionalism. Students begin by defining this for themselves with statements such as "demonstrate respect for the instructional team and peers by staying focused and not being distracted by digital devices." These kinds of agreements keep Viji from having to be the authority on setting rules that she would like to see in place. As students become accustomed to using the rules in real time, they will likely see the need to tweak some of them to be more specific as the course progresses.

What happens if a peer doesn't follow the rules? Students often need to be prompted to think about these kinds of situations and edit the agreements for consequences or ways to intervene. By brainstorming with students how to handle these situations, you can model your partnership in facilitating. Jay Howard's advice guide for "How to Hold a Better Class Discussion" reminds us that "Ground rules are also helpful when a student—intentionally or unintentionally— makes a racist, sexist, or homophobic comment" (Howard, 2019). In these situations, the instructor or the peers can remind the commenter about the rules of engagement, which hopefully contain a clause about not attacking individuals or making hurtful, stereotyping statements about a group of people. If the rules don't include words like this, the instructor can pause and use a few minutes to update the rules with the class.

Recall the situation at the beginning of the chapter in which an individual uses up a great deal of time during introductions, hijacking the plan, and resulting in a late schedule. When rules or norms are designed collaboratively and discussed explicitly, it makes it easier for a facilitator or a participant to redirect someone else's behavior. In short, it becomes easier to say, "I'm interested in what you're saying, but as timekeeper we're going to need to move on to our next person if we are to hear from everyone and keep to our schedule."

How Will You Keep Time?

We've all been in situations where we felt the group's time wasn't managed well, and it leads to frustration for everyone involved. Similarly, when someone hijacks a discussion you might wonder, "Why doesn't the meeting leader just cut them off kindly? Why is it so common for time to be mismanaged even when there is a clear plan?" Many facilitators are reluctant to take on the task of being a timekeeper. We think Hannah Feldberg-Dubin sums up being an effective facilitator perfectly: "Manage time like you're a referee" (Feldberg-Dubin, n.d.)

Like a basketball game, a class session is constrained to a finite amount of time. Keeping time is squarely the responsibility of the educator. Sometimes this means cutting off a good discussion or a particular dominating student, and this can be difficult. It is normal to feel uncomfortable about this. However, with the power dynamics that play out in a classroom, students are counting on their instructors to play this role so more students can be included. Alternatively, an instructor can let students brainstorm ways they can take on this timekeeping role with permission to signal or interrupt.

We are both in the habit of including time guidelines for ourselves in our class planning and we do our best to stick to them when interacting with students. For instance, we might plan one minute of silent individual thinking time, followed by three minutes of small-group discussion, finished off by a fifteen-minute large-group discussion. It's difficult to perceive time normally while teaching, so we set timers on our watches or phones and take the guesswork out of it.

Envision a noisy classroom with many small groups chatting away. You might wonder: How can I interrupt them and regroup? Some instructors use a chime or raise their hand in the air, tap a microphone, or do all three. In an online breakout session, it is easier when a message that they have a certain amount of time left gets sent to students. We find that interrupting lively conversations to start another one is both the joy and challenge of an inclusive and collaborative classroom. Admittedly, we were uncomfortable with this when we first began timekeeping more intentionally. Now we remind ourselves and our students that we are being inclusive by sticking to the timeline.

Are You Willing to Adjust the Plan?

If the discussion is rich, we may choose to bend our plan. We believe there should be room for this kind of flexibility, especially if we are building community and learning at the same time. A good facilitator will read the room and adjust accordingly. Picking up social cues likely entails looking at students' faces for expressions such as discontent, confusion, and wonder. Many instructors walk around a classroom looking at student work, listening to discussions, and talking directly with students. Because we both teach hundreds of students, using facial cues, and visiting most students can be challenging. We found quick techniques to read the room that can be helpful for small settings too, such as a physical "thumbs-up, thumbs-down" approach or a quick digital poll. These methods invite all students to give feedback to the facilitator. For example, when giving the students a problem to solve quietly on their own we might say, "if you have completed this already, give me a small thumbs up at your chest level." This allows us to monitor the thinking time needed, and it doesn't single out the students who process more slowly by saying, "raise your hand if you need more time." In our experience, we're unlikely to have complete consensus from 100 percent of our students, so we often set some threshold for when we will continue to work on a concept or move along. We aim to use transparent language about our pedagogical choices to students and help students who aren't there yet to find the resources they need to continue to use.

Do You Have Accessible and Clear Instructions?

You might have the best intention as a facilitator, but you will likely face hurdles if you don't provide accessible and clear instructions to your participants. We are both strong proponents of offering both visual and oral instructions (see discussion of Universal Design for Learning in chapter 2). Why? We learned from experience. When Kelly first began incorporating a lot of active learning, she would design an activity, tell the students what to do, and the very next thing many would do is turn to each other and ask, "What did she say?" It is easy to imagine that anyone's attention could be elsewhere the moment instructions are given verbally or that there was a nearby noise disturbance, or that someone might need to hear a prompt more than once. It's easy enough to display the prompt on a slide or in a handout, in addition to saying it. Multiple modes don't harm the students that are fine with only one mode, but it could be especially helpful to students with ADHD, multilingual learners, and students with hearing or visual impairments.

Sometimes students struggle with instructions because they don't understand the prompt or assignment. When we find ourselves clarifying our instructions over and over, we know it is time to revise the prompt for the next time. To bring as much structure to the prompt as possible, consider consistency with the prompt, timing expectations, and collaboration rules such as our example in figure 5.1. We find that consistently using a colored box on our slides, such as

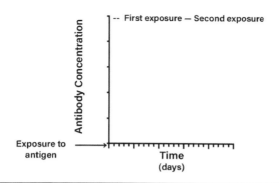

Draw a dotted line for an immune response for a person who is exposed
to a virus for the first time. Draw a second solid line for a different
person who is being exposed to the virus for a second time in their life.
- Draw your two lines alone (2 minutes).
- When prompted, compare your lines in your assigned group and
  justify your reasoning to each other (3 minutes).
- The group's reporter should be prepared to draw the group's
  consensus answer on a white board if the group is selected.

Figure 5.1. A sample activity with structured prompts (often within a colored box)
that instruct students with timing and collaboration expectations.

bright blue, helps students stay attuned to their task. It is a
simple way for students to quickly find the instructions they
need for activities.

Have You Considered the Physical Space?

One semester, Kelly and a colleague planned their course
to have students form permanent discussion groups in a
fixed-seating lecture hall. It required two students in one
row to turn around to speak to two more students in the row
behind them. You might guess that this was problematic.
Turning around was physically uncomfortable, and unless

Kelly prompted them every single time, students simply stopped discussing in groups of four. The example depicts how important the physical space is in our facilitation.

While each space will be different, we usually review a few things in any room for an in-person course. Does the furniture move? If so, does the room need to be set to a specific configuration for the specific type of facilitation planned? With movable furniture you might want to arrive early or provide instructions to students at the start of class to optimize your space for that day's class activities. If the furniture doesn't move, can I leave a row or two vacant for movement through the room? Will students be able to see my slides in this space? If the space is large, is a microphone available? These considerations allow more students to take advantage of the value of being in a room together. Many of us reaffirmed this value after teaching remotely during the COVID-19 pandemic.

How Do You Take Your Facilitation Skills from Good to Great?

In table 5.1, we summarize our six key questions for facilitators by examining sample scenarios and incorporating a more inclusive overlay. You will note that our theme of structure helps to distinguish the more inclusive approaches from the less inclusive ones.

Intentional facilitation is an important aspect of structuring an inclusive classroom. In Priya Parker's book *The Art of Gathering,* she discusses the invisible structure that is engineered to not only connect those who gather with the purpose, but also to connect them socially (Parker, 2020). By carefully reflecting on your role as facilitator and doing so with an inclusive overlay, you are reinforcing students' sense

Table 5.1   Six key questions for facilitating inclusively applied to example scenarios

	Example Scenario	Incorporating a More Inclusive Overlay
Do You Have a Plan?	The instructor wings it: They walk into the class session with three broad questions that they will have the students work through.	The instructor outlines three questions and may provide the questions to students in advance of the class session. The instructor has a plan for the method they will use (such as a think-pair-share or small group discussion with assigned roles for group members).
Do You Have Rules to Help Others Stick to the Plan?	The instructor sets no rules and the students are free to contribute (or not). Perhaps the syllabus outlines expectations for participation, but students aren't sure if they are adhered to at every class session.	The instructor either designs or codesigns with the class the rules of engagement for participation. Students are clear on how they will be evaluated in their participation and what will happen if the rules are broken.
How Will You Keep Time?	The instructor tells students to take a few minutes to talk to neighbors about a prompt. They do not give a warning when the few minutes are up, nor do they say what will transpire with the discussion. Some students take much longer than needed and others have not had their turn.	The instructor says, "You will have three minutes to talk with a neighbor. I will give you a one-minute warning. When time is up, I will randomly call on some groups to share your group's thoughts." The instructor uses a timer and sticks to the timeline.
Are You Willing to Adjust the Plan?	The instructor works through a problem and looks out to a sea of faces. Many appear engaged, but some look like they have checked out and may be on their computers or phones.	The instructor asks all students to give a thumbs up if the solution is clear or a thumbs down if the solution is unclear. The instructor determines what the threshold is for moving on (e.g., 90% are thumbs up) or discerning where students are stuck.

Table 5.1 Six key questions for facilitating inclusively applied to example scenarios

	Example Scenario	Incorporating a More Inclusive Overlay
Do You Have Accessible and Clear Instructions?	The instructor verbally asks students to do an activity, such as draw a graph, write a response, or discuss with a partner. Many students are not doing what the instructor asked or are asking the instructor and peers a lot of questions about what the task is.	The instructor provides both verbal and visual instructions. The instructor posts the question, the instructions for discussion, the timeline, and any additional information, such as how to introduce themselves to group members.
Have You Considered the Physical Space?	The instructor walks into the room and says, "find a partner or group of three to work with and answer a question posed on the board," without any consideration of how the seats are arranged or if the board is visible.	The instructor comes early to arrange the desks in groups of three and asks all students to join a group. Any groups of fewer than three will be asked to be a part of another group. The instructor circulates around the room to ensure that students are part of a group.

of community and belonging. Of course, we don't always facilitate perfectly the first time, or even the first few times. It will be important to consider how you will reflect on and revise your facilitation.

Frankly, when we are doing all these tasks as a facilitator, we find it difficult to effectively keep notes for ourselves about what worked and didn't work in real time. Viji likes to use her phone to dictate an audio memo when she walks out of the classroom so that she can revise for the next time she teaches the course. If you are using slides, you might make a few quick notes on the first slide. This can help you remember aspects that need to be tweaked if you use the same materials again.

Now, let's shift gears from thinking about the facilitator role to taking a look at some common activities we might incorporate in a class session and applying an inclusive overlay to them. How might we enact these techniques with inclusion in mind?

How Can You Bring an Inclusive Mind-set to Your Teaching Strategies?

One of the more influential papers to inspire our work has been Kimberly Tanner's article, "Structure Matters: Twenty-One Teaching Strategies to Promote Student Engagement and Cultivate Classroom Equity" (Tanner, 2017). It's a wonderful trove of techniques with tips on giving students time to think and talk, building community, and encouraging and managing participation from all students. We use Tanner's lens of structure in all of our work. As we outlined in chapter 1, we think of inclusive teaching as something to add to any strategy an instructor already uses by asking: "How can I bring more structure to this?"

In this section of the chapter, we've chosen strategies that we think most educators already use in their classroom interactions with students, and we hope we can spark ideas for improving structure. We are optimistic that the discussion will be able to nudge a few instructors to try something entirely new, too. We'll consider more structure and inclusion related to lecturing, think-pair-share, classroom response systems, whole-class and small-group discussions, and random calling. This is not an exhaustive list. By providing numerous examples, we hope to show that a similar set of tools and thinking emerges around how all students, from any background or demographic, can be better included.

Are You Lecturing?

What do you think of when you hear the word "lecture"? Is it a positive or negative feeling? It may be one of the most divisive words in higher education these days. For us, lecturing is a tool, but it should not be the only tool. When it is, we might call this kind of teaching "continuous exposition," as discussed by Derek Bruff, assistant provost and executive director of Vanderbilt University's Center for Teaching (Bruff, 2015). We agree with Bruff, who goes on to say, "Yes, I lecture, too. Just not continuously. A well-timed explanation can be very effective at promoting student learning." Recognizing that we all do some talking, explaining, and storytelling while our students are listening, and perhaps note-taking, what can we do to add an inclusive overlay?

What Are Some Visual Considerations?

If your lecture includes an accompanying visual display such as slides, we recommend investing time in learning about effective presentation design. One such book is *Presentation Zen Design,* by Garr Reynolds, in which we are reminded to avoid clutter on our slides, design text for the last row, and focus on storytelling, along with many other useful tips (Reynolds, 2012). Before a semester starts, Viji often goes to her empty classroom, pulls up a sample slide deck, and goes to different sections of the room to assess visibility. Suffice to say, we've probably all made mistakes for our colorblind and dyslexic students, but there are plenty of tips available for doing better. For example, putting a slide in grayscale will allow you to see what text or images need better contrast to aid colorblind students. We can help dyslexic students by using certain fonts that appear less crowded and using good spacing between words and sentences (British

Dyslexia Association, n.d.). Furthermore, many programs such as Microsoft PowerPoint offer an ability to check accessibility within the platform. Improving slide design will make learning accessible for more students.

We share another consideration about visuals and presentation because it is a pet peeve of ours. We observe this mistake often in classrooms and in other presentations. Imagine yourself showing students a famous quote or maybe giving instructions for active learning. Kudos to you, because you are following best practices with universal design—that is, making the information available with both visuals and your oral cues. In your imagination, are you reading the text exactly as it is or are you summarizing much of the text? Students will only stay attuned to your voice or the words on the screen, but not both well simultaneously. There are many outstanding resources for how multimedia can help or hinder learning, and we've learned much from Michelle Miller's book *Minds Online* (Miller, 2014). She suggests a "Goldilocks principle" with respect to the discrepancy between the visual presentation and narration. In other words, you don't want to read it verbatim, nor do you want it to be highly discrepant, but something in the middle with a conversational emphasis. Alternatively, if your slide is lengthy, you might ask students to read the slide silently to themselves, making sure you have accommodations for visually impaired students.

What Are Some Auditory Considerations?
A speaker is invited to the front of the room. A microphone is handed to them and they say, "No, thanks, I can project. Can everyone hear me?" You may have done this yourself or seen this common scenario and you'll likely see it in the future,

too. However, very few people can project for a sustained amount of time. When we think of a parallel scenario in a classroom with power differences, can we be certain that students are going to tell a professor if they cannot hear well? If a microphone is available, use it yourself and advocate that others also use it for presentations and discussions. As Jessie B. Ramey, a professor at Chatham University with hearing impairment eloquently states, "When you say you don't need a microphone, what you're really saying is that you don't care that I need you to use one. You are making the assumption that everyone is like you and can hear just fine" (Ramey, 2019).

Not only do individuals with hearing impairment benefit from the use of microphones, so do students who may be seated among chatty peers or multilingual students who can't afford to miss a word here and there. In short, using a microphone helps many learners. One of the benefits of using a microphone is that we are able to use our normal speaking voice, which can add to the authenticity of the experience. For example, Kelly is generally soft-spoken. The microphone allows her to speak in a conversational manner, helping students feel they know her as a person.

Beyond the microphone, remember that subtitles can provide visual cues that are helpful to all students as well. Use closed captioning on any videos shown in class and explore using closed captioning in real time with various slide presentation platforms.

What Strategies Assist the Notetaker?

In addition to these visual and verbal considerations, we also recommend providing structure to students taking notes. Not all students arrive at our campuses knowing how to take effective notes. Not all students are certain about the key takeaways from a lecture or how seemingly disparate pieces fit together conceptually.

How can we level the playing field for all learners? Some instructors provide a copy of the slides to students either before or after class. While we advocate that students should have access to these, they may not be the best tool for note-taking because they may not equip our students to assimilate the information in their own words. Providing a skeletal outline with certain pieces missing for students to complete as they listen would not only allow students to engage in note-taking but help scaffold the material in the manner in which the expert organizes the information. In their book, *Teaching and Learning STEM: A Practical Guide*, Richard Felder and Rebecca Brent aptly call this kind of tool "Handouts with Gaps." The gaps are places where students are asked to fill in more challenging material such as partial solutions, drawings, code, and processes either individually or in groups during class (Felder & Brent, 2016). We personally find we can accomplish a few goals with skeletal outlines. First, students learn how knowledge is organized. The organization of these outlines allows a novice to gain insight into our expert overview. Second, building resources like these convey that we care about their learning, and this goes a long way toward building rapport with our students. Third, we're building in lots of practice for retrieval of information, something we know from cognitive scientists is key to learning. Lastly, when we align our lectures to these skeletal outlines, we model for students how notes can be taken. We can help teach students effective note-taking strategies, no matter what our discipline.

Do You Intersperse Think-Pair-Share while Teaching?

We call the think-pair-share (TPS) technique the little black dress of active learning, meaning that it is versatile. Although TPS is easy to incorporate, it is often poorly executed. We've observed that many instructors skip the thinking part, and the class is immediately abuzz with discussion of the prompt. But what about students who need time to process the idea and construct their answers before jumping into a conversation? This may apply to introverts, students with learning differences, and multilingual students, to name a few. In a properly executed TPS, the instructor will prompt students to spend a specific amount of time thinking independently. This may sound like: "I will give you all one minute to think and write silently about the question. I will then prompt you when the one minute is up and you are able to talk with your partner about your ideas. You will have three minutes to discuss, and I will give you a one-minute warning before time is up. Finally, we will have ten minutes for a group discussion and I will share details of how that will be done later."

Besides providing explicit instructions for each phase of TPS, that structure may need to be enforced in the pairing as well. Simply stating "turn to a neighbor to discuss" might work for many students, but for some there is a realization that everyone around them has been paired up. Some students feel they are always the ones marginalized by peers in a class. Kelly reminds herself of what this feels like when she remembers always being the last one selected to join a volleyball team in middle school gym. It's uncomfortable to feel like the odd one out and that everyone else seems to have paired up or found a team except you. One way to avoid this is to assign students to groups or pairs that they can work with all the time. Assigning groups (with some student input or flexibility) is inclusive.

Let's think about another fitness-related example. Viji attended a gym where some work is often done in pairs. Without fail, the instructor asked for anyone without a partner to raise their hand and instructed those with raised hands to pair together. After the first few times of being embarrassed about not having a partner, Viji appreciated that there was an enforcement of this pairing. No one seemed to take it personally and it was a norm in this culture. How can we make this sort of inclusion routine in our classrooms? It may feel uncomfortable to ask if there is anyone in the room who doesn't have a partner. Instructors can circulate around the room looking for anyone who may need a group. When instructors aid pairing every time there is a TPS technique, students will begin to ensure that it happens without instructor intervention.

At some point, as has happened with us, students come to remark on how much they appreciate the enforcement of pairing. Consider some student feedback to assigned groups in Kelly's large introductory biology course:

- "I usually hate having to talk to people around me during lecture, but being put into a group with people you sit by all semester was great. You get to know those people and get comfortable talking with them."
- [working in groups in class] "Felt like a more even 'playing ground,' without groups consisting of friends who talked only to themselves."
- "I didn't feel like a burden on the people around me."

This last quote suggests that there were settings where a student felt that their presence in the classroom was a bother to others. While we can't know what led to that perception, we do not want any students hindered in their learning by that kind of feeling.

Finally, the last part of TPS is the sharing. In line with our continual emphasis on structure, we recommend having a plan and communicating that plan to your students. For example, you might advise students that you intend to call on a group/pair to summarize their discussion. More structure can be brought to the instructions by asking students to assign a reporter before they begin pairing (more on this later) and giving explicit directions about how much time a response should take (i.e., "in sixty seconds or less, share a few of your group's best suggestions"). Katelyn Cooper et al. review why whole-class share-outs can be problematic and provide some inclusive alternatives, such as one group sharing with another nearby, using polling technology, notecards, or shared electronic documents (Cooper, Schinske, & Tanner, 2021). Setting up the structure clearly and consistently will enable students to focus more on the learning and less on what will happen next.

Are You Using Classroom Response Systems (CRS)/Polling?

"I'll never go back to not using it in my classroom," one of our colleagues uttered after trying a classroom response system for the first semester. We wholeheartedly agree. Classroom Response Systems (CRS) are an essential component of our inclusive classrooms. A CRS is technology that allows the instructor to pose a question or poll to a group of students, and students respond via a digital device. The answers are compiled for the instructor, who may or may not share the answers with the students. Often, the instructor directs students to justify their reasoning with peers and then re-polls everyone before providing feedback. Derek Bruff's book *Teaching with Classroom Response Systems: Creating Active*

Learning Environments, is a good primer with practical tips on how to teach with this kind of technology, reminding us that "the technology used in classroom response systems is always changing, so any discussion of clickers that relies on features of current technologies is likely to be out of date soon" (Bruff, 2009). Note that even the term "clickers," popular when Bruff published his guide in 2009, is becoming an outdated term for this technology. Since 2009, the technology has mostly moved onto cell phones and laptops, thus offering more options beyond the original multiple choice question format. Nonetheless, as Bruff says in his new book, *Intentional Tech*, "We should be intentional in how we use technology, looking for ways technology can support student learning" (Bruff, 2019). Similarly, if our goal is inclusion, we should look for technology that supports this goal. Fortunately, CRS supports both learning and inclusion.

Why is a CRS tool so beneficial to learning and inclusion? When used regularly, effectively, and not optionally, it requires all students to synthesize material and apply it many times in a class session. This kind of practice aligns with what cognitive scientists know enhances long-term learning (Karpicke & Roediger, 2007). Plus, the constant formative feedback tells both the student and the instructor what a student might need to practice more. As for why the tool supports inclusion equally well (with a big assumption that all students have a device), let's revisit a passage describing a fictional student, Vanessa, whom we introduced in chapter 1. This scenario will allow us to consider how varied modes of participation can help more students succeed.

> Vanessa is a gifted student in a class with a Socratic approach. She's not comfortable raising her hand or blurting out answers

the way other students do. She's concerned that the instructor thinks she is not engaged.

If Vanessa's instructor used a CRS, Vanessa wouldn't have to raise her hand to answer. She and all of her peers could be equally invited to answer questions thorough their devices. Perhaps the reason Vanessa doesn't want to raise her hand is that she isn't confident yet and she doesn't want to be wrong in front of her peers. CRS technology allows her to engage with her instructor, while remaining anonymous to her peers. If the instructor combines the technology with peer discussions, Vanessa can work with just one or two other students, rather than taking a risk in front of the whole class. Over time, with many repeated questions, Vanessa will learn that her answers are on par or better than her peers' and will build the confidence she needs. This could cause her to engage more deeply with her peers and her professor and feel a better sense of belonging.

Over the years, we've both polled a huge number of students —hundreds of students and hundreds of questions each semester. We were recognized as such big users of one company's technology that they sent us each a box of gourmet cupcakes as a thank you (the perks nobody told us about in graduate school!). Over the years, we've compiled a few more tips around best practices for inclusion with CRS technology:

- Require participation from all students through the CRS (remember from chapter 2 why practice should not be optional). Grading need not be onerous and the score need not count for much of the final grade. Just be clear with students about how it counts. Various systems will allow you to decide if you want to grade some questions for effort only or if you want to add a value for correctness. Correctness might be tied to ensuring students are adequately prepared for class and can help regulate their learning (if they were tempted to skip the reading, for example). No matter how you execute it, grading conveys to the student that their participation is expected and valued.

- Don't ignore the responses/data. If too many students are not where you want them to be, don't move on. Don't be afraid to say, "I'm seeing that not enough students have this correct, so I'm not moving on yet."

- Use the poll-discussion-re-poll to say to students, "Wow, look how much learning just took place here" or "Here is the evidence that collaboration is powerful." Statements like these continually show your students how much you value learning and collaboration.

- Don't just tell students to "discuss" with their peers. When you do, you risk students saying something like, "I picked B, what did you pick?" Jennifer Knight et. al. evaluated the prompts instructors provided when posing a poll question, and they found that to promote rich discussion, the instructor should prompt students to justify their responses or provide a rationale each time (Knight, Wise, & Southard, 2013). Then, students can move beyond checking their responses to asking one another, "What was your reason for selecting B over C?" or "What's the difference between B and C?"

Are Your Students Doing Independent Work (Problem-Solving, Writing, Editing)?

There are likely times in class when you want students to be working independently. Perhaps they are problem-solving, responding to a prompt, editing, or diagramming. We're going to state the obvious here: when students are doing independent work, there should be silence in the room. Yet both of us have conducted several classroom observations and we have witnessed a consistent lack of silence during these moments. It's often not the students. Surprisingly, it's the instructor. We've seen instructors with best intentions allot time for silent work, but then they restate the question multiple ways or offer background discussion, which limits the time students have to do the work. It's worth noting: if you are asking your students to do independent work, stop talking!

Besides giving students the quiet time for thinking and processing, what else should you consider with this mode of teaching? As we discussed earlier, instructions for independent work should be made accessible and clear by being posted on a slide or other handout. Instructors can use the quiet time to circulate around the room to answer questions and provide encouragement to individual students. If students begin talking to one another during this designated silent time, we remind them that this is silent time, and let students know they will have time for discussion later. Lastly, be mindful of timing. Instructors tend to underestimate how long it takes to respond. We have a colleague in physics who advocates for the instructor to silently read the prompt and answer the questions, to make sure the minimum amount of time is given, while others may multiply the time it takes them by a factor of two or three. We both circulate around the room, observing how the work is progressing, and we sometimes poll them quickly to find out where they are in the task.

Do You Facilitate Whole-Class Discussions?
Leading an inclusive whole-class discussion is a challenge. Without structure, the discussion often takes a consistent pattern with certain individuals dominating and others unwilling to contribute. One study by sociologists found that on average, five to eight students contribute to 75–95

percent of most class discussions (Howard & Baird, 2000). This "consolidation of responsibility," in which just a handful of students participate, is especially true because participation is often optional. Jay Howard, a professor at Butler University, describes how this affects student behavior: "So long as students appear to be listening, they can expect that the professor won't call on them unless they signal a willingness to participate" (Howard, 2019). Howard's and others' research is beginning to give us a more complete picture of who is and who isn't participating as much as others in a variety of disciplines and courses. For example, in one study of whole-class discussions in introductory biology courses, females represented 60 percent of the students but their voices made up "less than 40 percent of those heard responding to instructor-posed questions to the class, one of the most common ways of engaging students in large lectures" (Eddy, Brownell, & Wenderoth, 2014). In a study of humanities and social science classes, discrepancies were observed based on age: students twenty-five and older were the minority in the population, yet they accounted for the majority of participation (Howard & Baird, 2000). These are just a few examples of differences that can be measured in classroom studies and they can perpetuate stereotypes about who is perceived as knowledgeable or engaged.

We often cite ourselves as examples of students not willing to contribute. Both of us were highly engaged students, but we never raised our hands to speak in our college classes. We assure you that we had many caring instructors, some of whom would be aghast to learn that we didn't feel comfortable speaking in their courses. For Viji, one of the challenges was not having time to formulate a thought while intently listening to others. In other words, she could have benefited from more silent time. For Kelly, it was anxiety about so much attention focused on her words. Interrupting someone was uncharacteristic for both of us, so navigating who would speak next when a discussion began to flow from student to student was another challenge. As adults, we still find jumping into academic discussions and meetings challenging at times.

One simple tweak to encourage more diverse participation is pausing to wait for more hands to be raised. Telling students: "I want to allow folks time to think and would like to encourage a broad set of students to participate. I will routinely wait until I see seven to ten hands in the air before I call on students." This technique is not only easy to implement, but also an elegant solution to helping you ensure silent thinking time and encouraging more volunteers to engage. Over time, more students will acclimate to this approach. We've observed colleagues who are similarly successful by stating, "There are some people I haven't heard from yet. I would love to hear from those people too." Neither of these approaches calls out quiet students directly, but they do provide encouragement. By stating your rationale to the whole class about wanting to hear from diverse voices, you are offering transparency in your commitment to inclusion.

If a whole-class discussion can be thought of as the main course, perhaps some students would prefer an appetizer to get started. Viji thought about this when she was given an assignment by an academic leadership coach. Because she found it difficult to speak up at meetings, despite having things to say, the coach assigned her the task of speaking up in the first few moments in upcoming meetings. It struck Viji as an odd assignment, but she obliged. The coach told her that her contribution didn't have to be a brilliant idea; even a clarifying comment or amplifying someone else's idea would work. By completing the exercise, Viji discovered what the coach already knew: an early engagement with the group enabled her to feel comfortable doing so throughout the meeting. What if we helped our students to engage early? A warm-up activity could give them an entrée into engaging in a whole-class conversation. It might be as simple as asking students to complete a sentence with one word or phrase in an ice-breaking activity that has no correct answer. If you use whole-group discussion routinely, consider an intentional warm-up activity to get all students prepared to engage.

The ideas above will help more students feel comfortable participating. As practitioners, we are continually asking ourselves, how can we have participation from all our students in a larger discussion? There are ways to jump-start discussions for every student, such as beginning with a TPS technique or a poll through a CRS. These techniques give students time to think and validate their perspective with peers before diving into a discussion. Another way to bring a diversity of ideas to a discussion is to ask all students to answer a prompt on a notecard. Students then swap the card a few times so that each student ends up with a card with an anonymous answer. Students volunteer to read the card they have because of its good content or, if uncomfortable with speaking to the class, they can indicate that they would like the professor to read it.

An electronic back channel is another approach is to bring in viewpoints. Many of us experienced how this could work during the COVID-19 pandemic, as students put thoughts and questions into the online chat while an instructor or peer talked. Expanding the discussion beyond the traditional means of "speaking up" indicates that all students' voices matter in the classroom, and that there are a variety of ways to contribute. Instructors may even be able to provide the nudge a student needs to speak up if they first read it to the class and then say, "I'm really intrigued by this thoughtful answer, I wonder if the author would be willing to reveal themselves and expand on it?" There will always be students who are willing to dominate a conversation, but when an educator structures a discussion, it allows everyone to see that good ideas abound in the classroom. The strengths of diversity are revealed.

Whole-class discussion is a strategy that may also reveal true differences in culture. For example, in a project at the University of Alaska to better understand how to be inclusive of Native Alaskans in their classrooms, researchers made this observation that is worth reflecting upon: "They hold an open space between voices. They make time for silence and reflection between overture and response. Even young people who have picked up their pace to match the dominant Western community tend to speak more slowly than those around them, to be more comfortable with silence, and to refrain from interrupting others before they have finished speaking" (Merculieff & Roderick, 2013). Having a conversation with your class about cultural norms in group conversations such as pausing, silence, eye contact, interrupting, or affirming others' answers aloud can be a fruitful way to acknowledge differences in how individuals may engage in a group context. Raising awareness about these differences and then moving toward having a common set of discussion norms for your group can help mitigate feelings of exclusion. In short, these norms provide structure and allow students to feel safe and welcome to contribute to the discussion in ways that you have collectively devised.

How does physical space make students feel safe and welcome in a discussion? It might be ideal to form a circle in a small classroom if the furniture allows. Large classes are often more limited in how the furniture can be arranged, but that doesn't mean we should ignore the physical space. For instance, if the classroom is larger than needed, blocking off every third row allows for the instructor to move closer to more students. Figure 5.2 shows Viji, photographed in a blocked-off row as she talks to a student.

Moving closer to students allows an instructor to repeat comments (word for word if possible) if a microphone isn't available to students, and to thank students for their contributions. During our conversations with students, we've learned that eye contact with instructors makes them feel included. Yet in a large classroom setting, it may be absent. We need to be cautious about getting too close to students for eye contact, too. Just as we discussed differences in the pace and pauses of conversation in Native Alaskans, eye contact is another physical component of facilitation with different cultural norms. For example, in East Asian culture, individuals perceive another's face as less approachable when direct eye contact is made, compared to individuals from Western European cultures (Akechi et al., 2013).

With so much diversity in a classroom, we may not be able to make all students feel comfortable with a whole-class, free-flowing conversation. Yet we can strive to make it a safe environment by starting with group discussion ground rules, providing positive reinforcement to comments made, encouraging early engagement, using writing, technology, and peers. When we cultivate a safe environment, students may grow out of their discomfort. Sarah Rose Cavanagh describes how this happened to her in classrooms in which she felt nudged, nurtured, and valued by her professors, "The first few times I raised my hand and contributed something, I couldn't hear myself speak at all, so loud was the roaring

Figure 5.2. Viji (*bottom right*) is in a blocked-off row so that she can more easily access students one-on-one in a lecture hall. Photo by Viji Sathy.

in my ears. I teared up. I probably turned scarlet. But I participated, and then I participated again. Each time was a little easier. I regained my lost voice. My experience maps perfectly on what psychologists know is the most effective treatment for anxiety: controlled exposure in a safe setting" (Cavanagh, 2019).

Do You Have Students in Small Groups for Discussion?
Research tells us that some students struggle with being part of small-group discussions more than others. For instance, Katelyn Cooper and Sarah Brownell studied a small group of LGBTQIA+ students who reported feeling discomfort in small groups for active learning (Cooper & Brownell, 2016). "The extra cognitive load of needing to establish whether group members might be accepting of one's LGBTQIA+ identity, debating whether or not to come out, and then going through the process of coming out means that frequently switching up groups during the term may lead to significantly more stress on LGBTQIA+ students that could detract from their learning." As is often the case in education, there are trade-offs to the decisions we make, and we must find room for flexibility for students. One takeaway from this study is that if assigned groups are used, keeping them for an extended time is preferable. Switching groups only a few times a semester minimizes the introductions yet helps to broaden community.

Researchers studying three large introductory biology courses observed that within peer discussions, female, historically underserved, Asian American, and international students all preferred to be a listener or collaborator, rather than a leader (Eddy et al., 2015). The reasons for the differences were not clear-cut, but the researchers note that "students face barriers such as anxiety about group work, low perceived value of peer discussion for their learning, or contending with other students in the group who are dominating." One of the concluding statements of the study includes our favorite word: structure. "Reframing inequities in participation in this way puts the onus on the instructor to structure the interactions in peer discussions to promote equal opportunities for all students to participate in the learning activity." We wholeheartedly agree. What can we do, as instructors, to help more students?

As more research becomes available on how diverse learners participate in active-learning peer groups, we continue to listen and learn, as well as build empathy for individuals and groups of students. We also remind ourselves that the goal is learning, and sometimes students may feel discomfort in the process of interacting with peers. As practitioners, we love the challenge of trying to apply the knowledge created by educational research. In this case, we think it's prudent to continue to provide structure, kindness, and flexibility to our students, as we utilize the power of peer-to-peer learning.

So, in what ways can you bring more structure to small-group discussions? Many of the ideas stated above for whole-class discussions apply here, yet there are a few additional aspects we often consider. Many students have worked in small, static groups in their years of schooling, but have usually not been given explicit instructions on how to maximize communication. We suggest taking class time to implement activities that help students get to know one another and teach students to write team agreements. To reduce inequities in participation, an instructor can assign roles to students within the group, such as reporter, recorder, timekeeper, researcher, etc. Roles can and should rotate, too. We both teach in lecture halls with fixed seating, so physical space is a factor to think about if students can't move around. In rooms with flexible furniture, we have to repeatedly direct student movement: "Please turn your desks around." More prompts may be necessary for productive work, such as "this is a time to put devices away" or "please be sure your name tents are visible to each other." Again, the goal is to provide structure so groups can move past barriers and engage in effective collaborative learning. If you leave it to chance, we know that some students may struggle more than others.

Do You Use Random Calling?

Imagine you are observing a colleague teach and they are using a variety of active learning techniques, such as classroom response systems, TPS, and small-group activities. After each of these activities, they bring the class back to a common experience, asking for volunteers to share their ideas or reasoning. This all sounds wonderful, right? Are they missing anything or anyone? Research demonstrates that certain student groups will be more willing to volunteer to share with instructors than others. Notably, research shows gender gaps in verbal whole-group participation (Eddy, Brownell, & Wenderoth, 2014; Aguillon et al., 2020). This is where random calling can bring more equity to who participates.

Of all the techniques used in a classroom, random calling draws the most anxiety and ire from students and perhaps the most discomfort for instructors, too. In this technique, the instructor has a list and randomizes the names of students or groups to share during whole-class discussions (and potentially after TPS or small-group activity). When employed successfully, random calling on individuals can increase the number and variety of students who answer a question (Dallimore, Hertenstein, & Platt, 2013). Even in the face of such evidence, it can be difficult to employ in a classroom setting. One specific study nudged Kelly to adopt random calling in her courses. After learning about it, she came to believe she wasn't just missing diverse voices, but potentially doing harm. In the study, researchers demonstrated that students who were frequently volunteering to participate were deemed "experts" by their peers, and across all classes, these experts were always males (Grunspan et al., 2016). Not wanting to create stereotypes of who is or isn't knowledgeable in her classroom, Kelly decided it was time to figure out a way to employ random calling in a way that felt comfortable for her and her students. In essence, she wanted to convey a message that all students can be considered experts.

Kelly and her introductory biology colleagues worked together on this issue over several semesters, knowing that if all sections of the course were similar, it would be easier for instructors and students to become accustomed to the practice. Kelly and her colleagues made decisions based on costs and benefits. Their feelings aligned with what Waugh and Andrews discovered when they interviewed instructors: "Random call users saw student anxiety as a potential cost of random calls, but thought this cost could be substantially reduced through specific components of their random call implementation" (Waugh & Andrews, 2020). Similarly, they settled on what they thought might be most comfortable: random calling a group, not an individual. Each semester, with hundreds of students, they assign students to small discussion groups and then randomize the group numbers on a spreadsheet. After each activity, they call on group(s) that are next on their list. They have seen greater engagement and accountability when they have employed these random call strategies, which can benefit learning. But there are more questions to consider. Who speaks up for the group? What if the volunteer for the group if more likely to be male, thus enforcing stereotypes they were hoping to counteract? Indeed, there is research showing that males are more likely to volunteer after group discussion (Aguillon et al., 2020). More structure can bring more equity. Here are a few more ways we bring more structure to random calling:

- Assign a reporter if using group random calling. We like to rotate these in fun ways so that students learn about each other in the process and we diversify the voices. We often use the phrase "the person in the group who ___ will be the reporter." We fill in the blank with ideas like whomever has the largest pet, closest birthplace, most vowels in their name, last ate a burger, birthday closest to today, and more. While students may not always follow, especially if someone in the group is very anxious about public speaking, structure increases the chance that diverse voices are heard.
- Be transparent about why the technique is being employed. We are always proponents for sharing research and your own philosophies about inclusion with students.
- Allow a student to say "pass" as part of the rules of engagement. Viji realized this needed to be a part of her course during a meeting. Participants were instructed to respond to a prompt. They went around the room and each person responded. It wasn't an easy question, and Viji felt deeply uncomfortable as it became clear her turn would come soon.

While thinking, she was also half listening, hoping not to repeat anyone's answer verbatim. Her face became warm and her heart pounded loudly, making it even more difficult to listen to others in the room. She responded but can't recall her response. What she does remember was that about the twenty-fifth person into this exercise said, "pass." She distinctly remembers the mix of feelings she had when she heard this individual say pass and then the facilitator moved on to the next person. She could have just said "pass?" The point of the story is that the rules of engagement weren't clear—and she vowed to make them clearer in her classroom.

For random calling, and any of the techniques above that involve a student sharing an answer, you'll need to be prepared for the answer to be incomplete, wrong, or irrelevant. It helps if you plan for this in advance and have a few positive key phrases in your back pocket that work for you. We dive into this a bit more below when we discuss "instructor talk." We advocate for always thanking a student for their contribution and then deciding the best course of action that will convey a growth mind-set (we learn from mistakes) and collaboration (we learn together). We find it is helpful to remind students that wrong answers are often misconceptions held by many students, and tackling the reasoning helps everyone correct the misconception. Our response to a wrong answer shows the collective value in hearing wrong responses and acknowledging that the answer is wrong, not the student. Through carefully chosen words, we as instructors can help all students feel like they belong, no matter what response they have shared. In our next section, we dive into a few more ways to create a sense of belonging when interacting with our students.

How Do You Give Students a Sense of Belonging?

A classroom is a community within many other levels of community (discipline, institution, higher education). Inclusion means helping all students feel part of the classroom community. Educators may take for granted the experiences and privileges they had as a student, making it difficult to know what others need to feel a sense of belonging and value. Many instructors in higher education were not taught how to design lessons and facilitate classroom interactions and even fewer learned techniques to foster belonging.

The feeling of belonging is powerful and has lasting impacts. Michael Dunlea, an elementary school teacher, reflects on this impact in an article on *Edutopia*: "About a year ago, I received a text in the middle of the teaching day from the mother of a student I had taught eight years earlier as a second grader. She thanked me for always being there for her son, who had come out as gay to their family the night before. She shared that her son—now a senior in high school—mentioned me in their conversation and said I had taught him that all people have equal value in the world, a lesson that helped him face the truth of who he was" (Dunlea, 2019).

There is no one way to help all our students feel they have equal value and belonging in our classroom and beyond, but there are a few considerations we'd like to reflect on for instructors to build classroom community. Perhaps, like Michael, we'll have an impact for many students far beyond our classroom and for years to come.

Do You Provide Opportunities to Share Pronouns?
Misgendering a person, incorrectly assuming a gender identity or using an incorrect pronoun, is often unintentional in a classroom. It is a hurtful offense, and it is often avoidable

on the part of facilitators. Unless you are certain you are using a student's chosen pronoun, we recommend avoiding pronoun use in class. Because of our large class sizes, we are usually unsure. We try to use first names or nongendered terms "your classmate" or "your team member." Helping peers to not misgender their peers is also necessary, but more difficult. Ask students to not make assumptions about others and provide a structure for students to optionally share their pronouns, perhaps on name tents (discussed below).

Do You Know or Try to Learn Everyone's Names?

Has someone ever called you the wrong name? Forgotten your name after meeting you many times? Pronounced your name incorrectly? Think about how you felt when this has happened or how you would feel. Names are an essential part of identity and belonging, so it is up to the instructor to have a plan to use correct student names and pronunciations during classroom interactions. In our very large classes, we both let our students know that we have a hard time remembering names, but that we improve with practice. (This doubles as a nice display of the growth mind-set we hope students will display toward our courses too.) To practice learning names, every time we summarize a student's response, we ask the student's name if we don't know it. Students see the effort and appreciate it. Research from Sarah Brownell's group demonstrates that the instructor doesn't need to know all the names for the majority of students to perceive that the instructor knows their name (Cooper et al., 2017a). We have both come to rely on name displays in our classrooms as essential tools. These can be placed on tables or hanging from lecture hall desks as pictured in figure 5.3.

The name displays allow students to choose the name

Figure 5.3. Students in a lecture hall with name displays on file folders hanging from their desks. Photo by Viji Sathy.

they want to be called and to optionally add a pronoun and phonetic pronunciation. This tool has become an essential part of our classrooms. We don't ever want a student to feel excluded because we didn't have a way of knowing the most important components of their identity. As Viji can attest, having grown up with a name that is unusual for many, when people care enough to get it right, it is noticed and appreciated. Be sure to pronounce it as they have shared it with you. If it is a name that is unfamiliar to you, you can say something along the lines of: "Did I pronounce it correctly? It's important to me that I get it right." Make a note for yourself so you don't have to keep burdening the student by asking to teach you again and again, which can be seen as a microaggression.

Are You Prepared to Interrupt Microaggressions?

Kevin Nadal, a professor of psychology and author of *Microaggression Theory: Influence and Implication,* gives us a succinct definition of microaggressions. They are "the everyday, subtle, intentional—and oftentimes unintentional—interactions or behaviors that communicate some sort of bias toward historically marginalized groups" (Limbong, 2020). Unwittingly, at some point in your time teaching, you will encounter a microaggression in a classroom setting. It will help to recognize such an event and be prepared (to the extent you can) to manage it immediately.

It may be beneficial to understand the type of microaggression that has occurred. Derald Sue et al. classified microaggressions of three forms (Sue et al., 2007):

- Microassaults: explicit verbal or nonverbal attacks meant to hurt someone (e.g., racial epithets, referring to someone as "colored" or "Oriental" or deliberately serving a white person before a person of color).
- Microinsults: verbal and nonverbal insults that carry hidden meaning (e.g., "you're probably good at math, you should do this part of the project," said by a white peer to an Asian student who is stereotyping all Asians as good at math, or two white students excluding the Black student sitting next to them during a small-group discussion).
- Microinvalidations: invalidating the experiences and existence of the victim (e.g., "I think all lives matter" during a discussion of Black Lives Matter).

In our classroom, we are likely to see the less conscious forms of microaggressions, the microinsults and microinvalidations. At times, these are extremely subtle and the offender may not realize the microaggression. There may be a temptation to ignore the microaggression, but as Tyrone Fleurizard says, "being passive—may communicate a lack of empathy and concern for the well-being of targets of microaggressions, in addition to communicating that denigration is normal." The best course of action is a direct but empathetic discussion (Fleurizard, 2018).

One approach is to press pause, so to speak, and say to your students: "Hang on a second, I'd like to take a moment to think about what just occurred." During that moment you can decide how to respond, and students are on alert that something transpired that requires attention. Calling out a microaggression can be uncomfortable to all parties, the person or people offended, the person who offended, as well as the instructor having to think on the fly about a response. You might use gentle approaches to confront the situation, such as discussing the difference between intent and impact. Here is a response that may be useful in a variety of situations: "You may not have intended your statement to mean _____, but it may have been heard that way by others and felt hurtful because _____. These things are difficult but let's not ignore this just because it's difficult. Let's see if, together, we can rephrase this." Cyndi Kernahan, in her book *Teaching about Race and Racism in the College Classroom*, discusses how she needs to accept the starting points of various students to help them learn difficult concepts. After a student made a comment in her classroom comparing the KKK and Black Lives Matter, she explains, "But by understanding the origins of his statement, I think I was able to respond with more clarity, less anger, and in a way that (I hope) addressed the broader misconceptions driving his comment" (Kernahan, 2019). We agree that as the educators in the room, we must acknowledge that our responsibility is to make teachable moments out of difficult comments and never back down from our role as facilitator. Our students hurt by microaggressions are counting on us.

Consider the perspective of a student who feels attacked through other students' actions and the impact of instructor intervention. Viji recalls a semester in a class of over 200 students where she encouraged students to think through a multiple-choice poll question. When the poll was completed, she made a remark that the class was very close to being 100 percent correct (i.e., all members of the class selected the correct answer). If this occurred the class would be celebrated in some way. At that instant, a student of color asked a clarifying question. Suddenly, some members of the class erupted in laughter, thinking that this was the student holding them back from getting 100 percent correct. Viji immediately knew the student was feeling called out by peers unfairly, and she knew she needed to say something. She stopped the class, to say: "Now, wait a second, it's a very good clarification question. It's extremely smart to be clear about this, since we'll see questions like this in the future and we'll build on this concept in the next few classes." The student approached Viji at the end of the class session and expressed her gratitude for her intervention and response. Viji acknowledged to the student that what had happened was inappropriate, and she would do her best to coach the class through better, more understanding approaches in the future. It was a small gesture, but the student was affirmed and understood Viji's commitment to including her, and every other student, in her classroom.

It will be important for you to brainstorm around instances like this in your classroom. Perhaps you can team up with a few instructors to role-play scenarios and how you might respond (you can use the Twitter hashtag #microaggressions to find examples). There are no right or one-size-fits-all answers, so we hope you spend some time thinking and planning for inevitable microaggressions in your classroom. Practicing phrases that interrupt microaggressions will make it easier. Lastly, if you are the one who commits the microaggression (it happens!) think about ways you can remedy the situation. If it feels appropriate to do so, be transparent with your students about how you were wrong and aim for better. Solicit their help in noticing and providing safe ways to communicate these with you, such as through an anonymous feedback survey that is always available.

Is Non-Content Instructor Talk a Part of Your Inclusive Teaching Tool Kit?

We'd like to share a construct that we have come to find very helpful in our work: non-content instructor talk. Kimberly Tanner's research group defined this is as "any language used by an instructor that is not directly related to the concepts under study but instead focuses on creating the learning environment" (Seidel et al., 2015). This is a broad definition, but we're most excited about this construct when we think about the ways this talk can support an inclusive classroom. For example, here's a phrase that promotes a growth mindset: "That's a really challenging concept. It's wonderful that so many of you now have a grasp of it." This one helps overcome imposter phenomenon: "You all belong here. I know that some of you are doubting that after this challenging exam, but I know that you will all improve, and I have no doubt you belong at this institution." For new teachers, it may be difficult to focus on instructor talk because the disciplinary content and skills are dominating one's focus. For experienced teachers, it might feel unnatural to make these kinds of statements and might take conscious practice and planning to sprinkle them throughout each class session. We continue to follow Tanner's work in this area, as this construct is a useful way to objectively measure non-content instructor talk in increasing feelings of belonging, promoting a growth mind-set, and more. We urge you to ask observers of your course to record when and how you use instructor talk, or simply record yourself and reflect on it. This kind of communication is likely to be just as powerful in correspondence to students via classroom announcements or emails. As experienced teachers, we know our careful, non-content instructor talk is the reason our students often comment at the end of the semester about how much they felt seen or cared for as a learner.

How Do You Continue to Cultivate Your Skills with Each Opportunity?

We know as teachers that our work is never done. Over time, the concepts and competencies we seek to teach our students will be in place and it will require less of our attention than it once did. Yet the best teachers see every semester and every student as an opportunity to learn about learners. In many ways, we see ourselves as akin to the coach of a team. As any effective coach knows, your number 1 responsibility is to develop individual talent, often for the collective good. We understand that the analogy isn't that simple, but it does help shed light on working with each student. In this chapter, we have focused on your role as coach by thinking about the facilitation skills and teaching strategies you use to maintain a safe and inclusive space for learning. When you do this well, you allow talent to develop from a diverse set of learners, some of whom may have never even been told they have talent before or who doubt themselves.

We never stop learning about how to interact with our

students because each student is an individual who has something to teach us about diversity. Consider a student one of our colleagues had in class. The student peppered the instructor with constant questions that were interesting, but they took the class in a direction that the instructor did not want to go. After a few instances of this, the instructor noted that many of the other students in this course with over a hundred students would shift or roll their eyes when this student's hand went up. The student was genuinely curious and eager to explore related ideas. Our colleague met with the student in office hours, and the student shared that they had high-functioning autism. Fortunately, our colleague was familiar with autism and recognized that this student needed more specific rules for this kind of social engagement. They worked out an agreement that the student could ask up to two questions in class and all others could be written down and passed to the instructor at the end of class. This plan empowered the student to use this strategy with their other instructors in other semesters, including Viji. From this student, we see why rules of engagement work better when they are specific and the specificity helps some students more than others.

Whether we meet a student with learning differences, one with severe visual impairment, a student from an underresourced high school, or a student lacking confidence, we learn that what helps this student often benefits other students too. In response to what we learn by meeting one student at a time, we make tweaks to our courses. These changes reach individual students in the future, even if we don't get to know them all personally.

We've covered a lot of ideas in this chapter. Remember that you can make incremental changes to your teaching.

We know all too well how hard it is to manage our own expectations about what we want to implement versus how many semesters it might take to get there. There are many opportunities outside the formal classroom to cultivate your inclusive practices, too. In the next chapter, we will discuss additional ways to reinforce your commitment to inclusion through interactions such as emails, your course site, and office hours.

INSTRUCTOR CHECKLIST

Facilitation skills:

- Have a plan for how students will participate and how you will facilitate as you build lessons.
- Consider guidelines and rules for discussion and co-create them with students.
- Tell students they will have a specific amount of time to think, write, and speak and set a timer so as to not rush this time.
- Read the room and adjust your facilitation as necessary by asking students to provide feedback.
- Be sure activity instructions are clear and accessible, perhaps in a colored box on a slide or provided on a handout. Include timing expectations and expectations around collaboration.
- Determine how best to use the physical space by arriving early to arrange desks, or have students help to arrange desks in a format that is best for the class meeting.

Common teaching strategies:

- Ensure that materials that are projected can be clearly read from differing points in the room.
- When lecturing, provide skeletal outlines for notes or have students share or swap notes to double as an opportunity to learn note-taking skills.
- Use a microphone in almost all situations.
- Enable closed captioning in videos and slide presentations.
- Assign students to groups or pairs. Circulate around the room to check for individuals who may not have a group to work with.
- Share expectations for reporting and time considerations in thinking or discussing material.
- When using a classroom response system or polling, specifically prompt students to provide a rationale for their answer instead of simply comparing answers with peers.
- Employ and safeguard silent time so that all students have time to think individually before speaking.
- In whole-class discussions, collect responses from more people by providing more wait time and encouraging words. Think about warming up to a whole-class discussion with small-group discussions first.
- For small-group discussions, add structure by assigning students to groups and roles within these groups.
- Random calling is a helpful technique that can allow students to identify multiple experts in the classroom but can also be deeply uncomfortable. Consider ways to make it more comfortable by providing structure and expectations for when this technique will be used.

Other techniques to provide students a sense of belonging:

- Use correct pronouns or skip them all together by using students' names or using a generic term like "student."
- Commit your students' names to memory (or at least some of them), use name tents, or ask students their names before they speak. Pronouncing names correctly is equally as important, so ask students to add phonetic spellings to name tents.
- Respond directly and immediately to microaggressions. It helps to have some tactics rehearsed so that in the moment you feel comfortable using them.
- Provide ways that allow students to share microaggressions you or others may commit.
- Use non-content instructor talk to coach students through the cognitive challenges, let all students know you care about their learning, explain your philosophy on inclusion, and more.
- Any approach or tool you use in class can be viewed through the lens of inclusion. Ask yourself: "Who is being included and who is being excluded by the choices I make?"

CHAPTER 6

INCLUSIVE PRACTICES OUTSIDE THE CLASSROOM

Peter Felton, the executive director of the Center for Engaged Learning at Elon University, uses the phrase "relentless welcome" to describe how institutions can go beyond an initial welcome to build relationships and help students succeed (Felton, 2019). As educators, can we relentlessly weave the idea of inclusivity into the day-to-day work that we do, such as email communications, our office hours, training others, grading, writing assignments, and more? We are constantly learning from others about incorporating inclusion in various aspects of teaching and encourage you to do the same. In this chapter, we touch on a few ideas to give you a sense of how we can weave inclusive practices into some of the activities that occur outside our classrooms.

How Can We Communicate Inclusion over Email?

What amount of instructor time is spent reading, deleting, and responding to emails? We've seen Twitter conversations about trying to quantify the average time faculty spend on different tasks but suffice it to say a lot of time is spent dealing with email (McKenna, 2018). Faced with a never-ending stream, some instructors might be tempted to answer students with curt and efficient emails. We've seen comments that many instructors strongly dislike receiving emails from students without a salutation, such as "Dear Dr. X," yet ironically, busy faculty often reply to students without a salutation and just get to the point, as illustrated below:

Subject: Assignment

Dear Dr. Flintstone,

I am really enjoying your class. I just wanted to ask you a quick question about our upcoming assignment. You said it would be okay if we interviewed a family member, right?

Sincerely,

Lee R.

Subject: Re: Assignment

Correct, as I said in class.

-Dr. F

Sent from my iPhone

After receiving this message, Lee will probably never email this professor again, and perhaps will not reach out to other professors. They might miss out on opportunities to form relationships, something we know can make all the difference in student success. If rushing can lead to interactions like the one above between Lee and Dr. F, it is useful to think about ways to be both efficient and welcoming to students, especially during the busiest times of the semester. Below are some suggestions that help guide us toward more inclusive communications via email.

Are You Using Names and Modeling Inclusivity?

- Use the student's name. Research shows how valuable this is to students in our classrooms (Cooper et al., 2017), so we need to continue to work on this outside the classroom too. Copy and paste it to be sure you are using the correct spelling, capitalizations, and accent marks.
- Model inclusive language in your email signature to demonstrate your values around inclusivity. A standard feature in email programs is to customize a signature that is placed at the bottom of outgoing messages. Adding pronouns under one's name signals to others that you don't make assumptions about gender identities and respect others' identities. Similarly, including information about how to pronounce your name indicates that you not only value learning people's names but honor saying names correctly. Viji uses a hyperlink ("How do I pronounce my name?") that takes the reader to an audio file of her saying her name (if you are wondering, her first name rhymes with "bridgey"). We've seen other useful customizations in educator signatures, such as quotes that reflect their values, a link to helpful resources, a web page, office hour information, and links to a calendar for setting up meetings.

Are You Conveying a Warm and Helpful Tone?

- Avoid language that can shame a student. In the earlier example, "as I said in class" implies you should know this and is equivalent to finger-wagging.
- Consider a closing such as "Best," or "Thanks for reaching out," before your name. You can make these an automatic feature of your email as a standard signature or create a shortcut that will expand to an appropriate closing such as "Thanks for your note, Dr. F" or "Looking forward to seeing you in class, Dr. F."
- Use autoreplies effectively. While it is common for people to put up autoreplies when they are traveling, autoreplies can also save a lot of time during busy periods like registration and the end of the semester. Recall that a friendly tone in your syllabus introduces the instructor as being warm and approachable. The same applies to your autoreplies during the semester. We have seen colleagues use autoreplies that answer frequently asked questions or a link to a web page that is helpful to students. If you can anticipate some of the common student questions or concerns and include them in your autoreply, you can potentially save time spent in answering repetitive emails, leaving you fresh for individual issues.

Are You Reaching Out to Individual Students?

- Email individual students that you would like to reach about certain issues, such as those who are struggling with graded assignments, those frequently missing deadlines or classes, those who are not thriving, or those who have made big improvements. Doing so not only signals that you are keeping tabs on their progress, but it can also help the student see you as a partner in their learning.

- Condense individual students into groups, if need be. If the choice is between not having the time to send ten emails to ten different students who have made improvements or bulk messaging them in a group, always choose the bulk email. (Don't forget to use the "bcc" option, which prevents people receiving the note from identifying others who also received it.) Some platforms make it easy to send the same message to a group of students and add a personal name to the top, but this isn't a standard function. Since we teach large courses, we typically opt for a bulk, bcc'd email. We find that students often write back about how honored they were to receive a message like this from a busy instructor. Even if it is a generic email to a set of students, you might try using phrases like: "I noticed that" or "I am happy to speak with you at office hours" or "I appreciate your effort in this course." These kinds of phrases help an email to a group feel personalized and convey care for the individual student.

How Do We Build Transparency and Structure during Office Hours?

Danielle Slakoff, a criminology professor at Loyola, mentioned in a tweet something we've seen others express: "I am rebranding 'office hours' into 'student hours' today. As a first-gen student, I was terrified of 'bothering' my profs. I hope this will help students feel more at ease" (Slakoff, 2019). Slakoff picked up the tip from someone else on Twitter, as many of us do. As is our mantra, we ask: "Who is being left behind when there is a lack of structure and clear expectations?" Many students, including first-generation college students, misunderstand what office hours are and what happens during them. As Anthony Abraham Jack shares: "The students who are least likely to go to office hours are the students who would benefit from them the most," as they become spaces where professors transform into advisors and mentors (Nadworny, 2019). We know that some students think that office hours are for asking questions or seeking clarification on content, but they don't always know if their questions warrant a visit or if office hours will be busy with other students. Some students may be fearful of visiting office hours (Nadworny, 2018). With a bit more intentionality and structure, we can demystify the traditional office hours, make them more flexible, and invite more students in to help bring equity in office hour participation.

Are You Demystifying Office Hours to Create a Welcoming Environment?

Viji uses a graphic in her courses to demystify office hours and show students the varied formats she uses. As can be seen in figure 6.1, she uses office hours that vary in format, duration, and location. She was inspired to do this when she noticed a pattern while talking to students during office hours. Some students revealed that hers was the first office hour they had attended (many of her students are in their second or third years). When she probed to understand why, many said they didn't know what they were for or didn't feel they could attend if they didn't have a specific question about the course content. As a result of these conversations, Viji added structure that would help explain what office hours could be used for through the graphic. While she did not rename her office hours, she provided details that would help students understand what could be discussed in these meetings.

Many instructors lament that students are not utilizing office hours. Yet we know how important personal

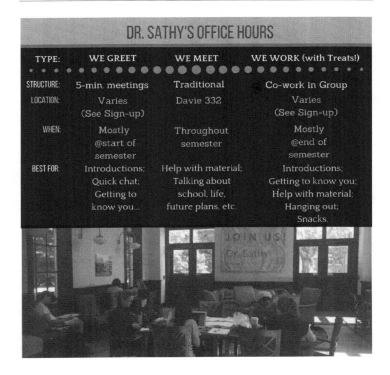

Figure 6.1. A graphic from Viji's syllabus helping to explain the structure of her various office hour formats to students.

relationships with professors are in student success (Kuh & Hu, 2001). If we understand why students do not attend office hours, perhaps we can we make changes that capture more of them. A study in 2014 by Griffin et al. surveyed over 600 students to learn what factors did and did not affect whether they attended office hours (Griffin et al., 2014). Somewhat surprisingly, whether a professor was approachable or available was not a significant factor in this exploratory study, but the convenience of time and location and the usefulness of feedback were significant factors.

Where Are Your Office Hours?

The location of office hours seems to matter somewhat in whether students find them convenient. Some students may be intimidated by being in an instructor's office, as a definite power dynamic is exposed. In his book *Together: The Healing Power of Human Connection in a Sometimes Lonely World*, Vivek H. Murthy recounts the experience of paying a visit to a patient at her home (Murthy, 2020). He notes how much more he learned from her in that short encounter and how comfortable she was there instead of at a doctor's office. It's not hard to imagine why a student may find it intimidating to come into our space to discuss their academic work. We've heard many ideas from colleagues about office hour locations, including student-focused areas like student unions, cultural centers, and libraries, as well as outdoors to the track for some "walk and talk" time. Online office hours also provide a convenience. Holding office hours virtually to meet students where they are, quite literally, can go a long way in reducing barriers to visiting us.

While there are many good reasons to hold office hours outside our office, there are times when we need a private location where a student can share confidential information about themselves, such as accommodations or grades. Building a welcoming space is important. We encourage instructors to walk out of their office and then back in, pretending to be a first-year student, for example, and ask: what impression am I making? Here are some things we've noticed over the years that make our offices welcoming:

- On our campus, we can complete training sessions related to student success and receive stickers we proudly display on our door (such as first-generation college student advocate or LGBTQIA+ ally).

- We usually have candy in a jar and tissues on hand. Over the years we are thankful for a never-ending supply of these. We've also seen faculty on Twitter post that they have a drawer full of energy bars that they offer to students, as they suspected many of their students could be managing food insecurity. These small acts convey much care and empathy for students.

- We have photos of our kids, pets, and other personal objects to help students see us as people. Viji has a wall of photos with former students in their commencement attire to help convey that these relationships continue beyond the end of a semester. Kelly limits the number of diplomas, awards, or other kinds of wall hangings that can intimidate a student. Note that this will need to be adjusted based on how you wish to convey who you are to your students in conjunction with how they may perceive you. For example, an instructor who is perceived as young may wish to post their diplomas and awards to help convey their credentials. There is not a one-size-fits-all here, so focus on how you might humanize your space in a way that feels authentic to who you are and won't undermine your authority.

- Lastly, we think about the layout of our offices. We try to avoid having a monitor or other obstructions between us and the student. If there's room, we try to set the chairs facing each other, as we might sit at a café. Placing a wall clock behind the student helps us politely keep an eye on time without having to look at our phone or wrist. If you share an office space with others, consider a rotating schedule to allow each other privacy for time with students.

When Are Your Office Hours?

The timing of your office hours will certainly include or exclude certain students. Varied times become necessary, as does the ability for a student to make an appointment outside of routine office hours. We also want to encourage you to make appointments with your students. While open office hours without appointments may work sometimes, they can often end up with a student standing outside an office for forty-five minutes, waiting for others to come and go. Online scheduling tools are more efficient for students and send a message that their time is important too. This has the added benefit of lowering one barrier to participation that we often hear about from students—because we teach large classes, they assume our office hours would be packed. A scheduling system makes your availability transparent. As a bonus, it allows for a digital trail of your visits and can be helpful as you consider your evaluations of the student for the course or future letters of recommendation.

How Useful Are Your Office Hours?

We recommend learning more about what makes for excellence in tutoring, such as the INSPIRE model shown in table 6.1 based on work by Lepper and Woolverton (Lepper & Woolverton, 2002). Wood and Tanner make a case that these are useful ways to teach our courses, modeling each class session as an excellent tutoring session (Wood &Tanner, 2012). Another way to improve your one-on-one work with students is the academic-coach approach, in which you help a student more holistically with issues such as time management, goal setting, and finding resources, as well as simple active listening techniques (Zenger & Folkman, 2016; Ohlin, 2020).

Is the biggest problem that office hours are *optional* for students? Plenty of approachable professors are holding

Table 6.1 The INSPIRE model of expert tutoring and results for tutees

Characteristics and behaviors of expert tutors	Results for tutees
Intelligent: Superior content as well as pedagogical content knowledge	Difficulty of questions optimally matched to students' levels of understanding
Nurturant: Establish and maintain personal rapport and empathy with students	Feeling accepted, supported, and free to explain their thinking
Socratic: Provide almost no facts, solutions, or explanations, but elicit these from tutees by questioning	Constantly thinking, doing, and responding
Progressive: Move from easier to progressively more challenging cycles of diagnosis, prompting toward a solution, and posing of a new problem	Moving in small steps to higher competency through deliberate practice
Indirect: Provide both negative and positive feedback by implication; praise solutions, not the student	Working in a nonjudgmental atmosphere
Reflective: Ask students to articulate their thinking, explain their reasoning, and generalize to other contexts	Gaining insight into their own thinking through metacognitive reflection
Encouraging: Use strategies to motivate students and bolster their confidence (self-efficacy)	Experiencing productive learning and gaining confidence in their abilities

Source: Reproduced by permission from Wood and Tanner 2012.

office hours in the student coffee shop ready to welcome a diverse group of students and offer useful feedback, and yet they are sitting alone. (We see memes about this, so it must be true.) If students don't do optional, how can we bring more structure for the students who might benefit most? Should all students be required to attend office hours at least once? Some universities have a first-year University 101 course that introduces students to helpful resources around campus. On our campus, students in this course have an assignment to visit at least one instructor's office hours. We value this course and the office hours assignment because it brings equity to knowing how to do college. As individual instructors, might we do the same? What would it look like in a larger class to require each student to attend office hours at least once? Here are some ideas for implementing this in any size class.

- Use a scheduling tool and require students to sign up for a slot that matches their availability (this could be part of a participation grade).
- Provide both in-person and online options.
- Allow students to come in pairs or small groups so that they are at ease. This has an added benefit of allowing you to efficiently meet more students.
- Try five-minute required meetings at the beginning of the semester to encourage students to become repeat attendees on their own.
- Provide useful advice or feedback during the first meeting so that students see the value of visiting office hours again.

How Can You Add Structure to Your Conversations with Students?

Just as physicians keep charts on their patients, we can collect lots of useful data about our students before they come to office hours that can provide useful discussion points. To make students feel welcome, we can start the conversation with questions about fun facts we might have gathered in a survey. For example, on the first day of class, Kelly collects information via polling technology about what county in North Carolina (or other state or country) students are from and one skill they have. She uses a spreadsheet generated from these questions to begin a file on each student. As she meets with them at scheduled appointments, she pulls up the information as a conversation starter and adds more notes about each student after the visit to help her keep track of their conversation.

Even if you don't feel particularly skilled with one-on-one interactions, we think it is your role as an educator to get the conversation started in an inviting way before moving on to business. In other words, how can we make the interaction seem less transactional and help put all students at ease? Some questions we keep in our back pocket as conversation starters:

- Where's home for you?
- What kinds of things do you like to do in your free time?
- What was one of your favorite courses last semester/in high school and why?
- How did you decide to come to [insert school name]?
- What are you considering as your major? (Occasionally, if the student seems open to it, you can ask about goals or plans after college, but this can be an unnerving start for some students.)

In general, having about a dozen or so questions of this type at the ready helps ease the student into a conversation. We aim to find commonalities with the student and keep the encounter from seeming like a one-way interrogation. When Viji realizes that she is dominating the conversation with her questions, she invites the student to turn the tables: "What questions do you have for me? It doesn't have to be about the content."

At times we may not have to start a conversation because our students may have a specific question or request for us. It is important not to lose track of time and miss the chance to address that question. If you are using a scheduler, you can ask students to post a question or comment in the meeting appointment ("just to chat," "questions," or "introductions" are possible options students can choose).

Lastly, if the student is requesting something that cannot be done during the meeting time, such as a letter of recommendation or information about a campus resource, make good notes about the request and tell them when you might have an answer. For good measure, suggest that they shouldn't hesitate to contact you again if they haven't heard back by a certain date. By doing these things, we are providing structure and transparency to the student about how we like to work on such requests and revealing this aspect of the hidden curriculum.

How Can We Create and Assess Assignments Inclusively?

Are You Using Assignments to Bring Diversity, Equity, and Inclusion to the Fore?

At times, it can feel challenging to find time in class to devote to issues of diversity and inclusion. For example, the Black Lives Matter movement has compelled some academics to say that addressing issues of systemic racism belongs in every antiracist classroom. Meanwhile, we've heard from colleagues who say they aren't sure how to broach issues of diversity, equity, and inclusion in their course or that these issues aren't relevant. We believe that every course offers an opportunity to engage in discussion about systemic cultural issues such as racism, sexism, and ableism, if the instructor is interested. One way to execute this is through course assignments.

Educators can design assignments with topics of diversity,

equity, and inclusion topics in mind. For example, in a biology course students might engage with a published case study about an athlete who is hormone tested and then denied the option of competing as a female (Vandegrift & Dawson, 2016). Students learn about androgen insensitivity and what determines a person's sex and gender identity. In statistics, students might analyze data on quantifying systemic racism, or measuring implicit bias, or any number of ideas or data sets that allow them to apply principal quantitative skills. While it may be more difficult to imagine how to include these topics in some disciplines, we've seen a lot of our colleagues sharing ideas to help one another move in this direction.

Beyond designing assignments on your own or with colleagues, you could take an inclusive and collaborative approach with students. Invite students to nominate topics or allow them to have some autonomy periodically to choose a topic of interest to them. For example, Viji recalls a project she completed as part of her introductory statistics course when she was in college. The instructor had students work in teams to develop a survey and collect data. However, for the analysis and write-up, the instructor encouraged team members to pose questions of interest to them individually. Viji dove into the project, investigating trends related to the model minority myth, while her peers examined other aspects of the data that interested them. This was the first time she recalls getting immersed in a line of inquiry that felt personally relevant in a quantitative subject. By giving her autonomy to select a topic of interest in this introductory course, the instructor allowed Viji to pursue more lines of inquiry, which ultimately became her first step in becoming a quantitative psychologist.

While we may be well-intentioned in designing our

assignments to incorporate diversity, equity, or inclusion, it is important that students not feel called out or that the assignment itself reinforce harmful stereotypes. Perhaps there are others who can review your proposed assignment and provide feedback. Are there peers, graduate students, or undergraduates who can conduct this review? Is it possible to consult with a campus organization (such as the LGBTQIA+ center in the example of biology case study above) to help you frame the assignment and readings that lead up to the work? These kinds of assignments can be sensitive, so we encourage you to draw on your networks to try to get it right.

Lastly, we encourage you to find scholarly work that is either conducted by underrepresented faculty in your disciplines or work that examines issues such as inequity, racism, sexism, and ableism as part of your assignments. Many organizations (e.g., American Psychological Association, 500 Queer Scientists) are collating lists of scholars who are minoritized in our fields, alongside resources for teaching. These lists can be a good place to start. We should not rely on a single course in a curriculum where these issues may be at the forefront for students. We can aim to ensure that every student is engaging regularly in discussions and work that allow for interrogation of how we know what we have come to know in our disciplines, and who has not had space to shape the field (Kwong, Sofia, & Ramirez, 2020).

How Are You Reducing Bias in Your Assignment Grading?
No matter how much we aim to be fair in our assessment of student work, it is important to acknowledge that our own conscious and unconscious biases may shape how we perceive and grade students (Malouff & Thorsteinsson, 2016;

Malouff, Emmerton, & Schutte, 2013). To mitigate against bias, consider techniques like:

- Grading blindly with names of students withheld. It's important to note, however, that it may not always be possible to grade blindly (personal essays, for example).
- Incorporating rubrics to apply feedback and points equitably. Typically, a rubric is a matrix that provides scaled levels of achievement for a set of criteria or dimensions of quality. There are many outstanding resources available to help build rubrics. For example, there are models of rubrics such as VALUE (Valid Assessment of Learning in Undergraduate Education), developed and led by the Association of American Colleges and Universities (AAC&U) that can help determine whether and how well students are meeting the learning outcomes in written communication, oral communication, information literacy, reading, and teamwork (Association of American Colleges and Universities, n.d.). Additionally, there are online rubric builders that can make quick work of this task (Allen & Tanner, 2006; Kharbach, n.d.). Besides setting expectations, rubrics provide transparency to students and provide a checklist so they can meet your expectations of the work.

Are You Providing Feedback Inclusively?

In 2013, a study called into question the practice of grading with red pens (Dukes & Albanesi, 2013). Undergraduate volunteers were asked to evaluate graded comments by an unknown instructor. When the volunteers did not agree with the comments, they judged them much more harshly when written in red as opposed to blue pen. The authors compared the perception of instructor comments to a physician's bedside manner. The results of this study hint at the multitude of subtle ways students receive messages from educators (and explain why Kelly was asked to supply blue and purple pens to her kids' school teachers, and not red ones).

Besides pen color, it is important to reflect upon other ways the delivery of feedback conveys implicit messages. "REWRITE this!!!" or "Do you even speak the English language???" are intimidating comments that our friends received when they were students. The fact that middle-aged people can still remember the sting of such comments tells us that the tone of the feedback matters. It is important to not take shortcuts on conveying a positive, growth-minded tone for all students.

Conveying high standards is another important part of inclusive feedback. In a double-blind, randomized study by Yeager et al., the researchers had middle school and high school students draft an essay, and their own teachers provided specific constructive comments (Yeager et al., 2013). Along with the comments, some students received a note with feedback, such as "I'm giving you this feedback because I have high expectations and I know you can reach them." Other students received a standard note: "I'm giving you these comments so you will have feedback on your paper." While the different type of feedback didn't yield large differences for white students, it significantly impacted African American students. These students were more likely to revise their work if they received feedback about high expectations (72 percent) compared to the standard comments (17 percent). Thus, being explicit about high standards will not harm the students who do not need to hear it, but it can be valuable to a student who may doubt their ability to succeed or distrust a system that reinforces negative stereotypes about their academic work.

An inclusive course will, in its very design, incorporate many opportunities for practice. That practice needs to be accompanied by helpful, timely feedback in an easy-to-understand format. Fortunately, there are many tools to help with immediate feedback to closed-ended questions (such as multiple choice, select all that apply, fill in the blank) but there are fewer robust tools for feedback to open-ended assignments (such as long answer, essay, papers). We encourage you to consult with your campus center for teaching about providing feedback at scale for your courses. Additionally, there are alternate grading approaches that emphasize a growth mind-set for students such as allowing revisions without overwhelming both the student and instructor in workload (Talbert & Clark, 2021). Frameworks like specifications grading (Nilson, 2015) or leveraging technology for feedback (Fiock and Garcia, n.d.) can help expedite the process, allowing for an optimal match between students and instructors on feedback (Mulliner & Tucker, 2017).

How Can We Create Inclusive Exams?

Much of what is outlined above applies to exams, quizzes, and poll questions too. Recognizing that assessments can take many different forms in different courses, we'll hone in on one of the most frequently used formats—high-stakes exams. We choose to focus on exams because they often serve as gatekeepers to disciplines, especially in STEM courses.

How Can You Set the Stage for Success?

A high-structure course will include frequent formative assessments (such as minute papers, poll questions, quizzes, assignments) that are aligned with your summative assessments (exams, papers, projects). In other words, students should not be surprised by the type of questions that you will ask in a summative assessment. Kelly learned this lesson early in her teaching career when she saw that students' feedback about her exams characterized them as tricky. Tricky can mean at least two different things: it can signal that there is intent to mislead the student based on the wording or answer choices, creating mistrust between student and teacher (see more on this below), or it can refer to a lack of alignment between classroom activities and the exams. She wanted her students to be able to answer tougher, more application-based questions, but realized that she hadn't been incorporating enough opportunities to practice these, so that students were prepared for them. Below are some questions to ask yourself, alongside concrete tips for preparing your students for exams:

- Are you using exam-caliber questions in your practice settings? We like to use the term TTQ, which stands for Typical Test Question. Kelly copied this from her high school calculus teacher, Joan Vas. Labeling questions in formative feedback (such as assignments, poll questions, quizzes) as TTQs helps students identify the caliber of questions they might expect to see in an upcoming exam.
- Are you aligning your formative assessment question types to those on higher-stakes exams? For example, don't use all open-ended formative assessment questions and then only multiple-choice questions for exams. Thinking about the principles of backward design, how can you best prepare students for your summative assessment? Practice. Practice. Practice.
- Can you provide practice exams that are similar in length and difficulty to the real exams? If you can, release prior versions

from a different semester and assign them. These practice exams can help ease anxiety for students.

- Are you using a grading scheme that allows for the occasional misstep? An exam that is worth a substantial portion of the grade can wreak havoc on a student's grade if they have one bad day. Additionally, we have learned from some students that a single bad exam score could falsely signal to a student that they are not cut out for work in our disciplines. There are many sound reasons for considering a grading scheme that allows for the occasional misstep. For example, in our STEM disciplines, we often discuss the importance of failure and learning from it. However, when we looked at our grading scheme, we realized that we had not put this into action by allowing for a low quiz or exam score to be dropped. Viji decided that she wanted to show her students how important a growth mind-set was by indicating that the cumulative final exam could replace one of the mid-semester exams if students did better on it. It allowed for students to get a do-over; they also stayed motivated to learn the content in the hopes of demonstrating proficiency of the material at the final.

Are You Constructing More Inclusive Exams?

It may not surprise you that there are people who get PhDs in assessment, test construction, and test analysis. Viji happens to have one of those PhDs and she will readily admit that test writing is among the hardest tasks she does. Why is it so hard? It is difficult to come up with questions that don't simply rely on recall of facts or are nearly identical to prior practice. Ideally, students will demonstrate transfer of learning by applying knowledge and skills to a novel question. Below are some questions you can ask yourself to help make your assessments more inclusive:

- Can you be flexible on the schedule? Is it necessary to administer an exam synchronously and in-person? If not, you can allow students to take the exam that is ideal for them. Take-home exams are a good example of this and something many educators became more familiar with during the COVID-19 pandemic. You'll likely want to offer some guidelines about how long students might expect to work, as well as any resources that are acceptable to consult.

- Can you incorporate aspects of nontraditional testing in your exams? For example, two-stage exams are gaining popularity among educators as a means of assessing student work and improving student learning (Zipp, 2007). In short, students work independently on an exam and it is collected or submitted (round 1), and then the exam or portions of the exam are released again (round 2) for students to work on collaboratively. These two scores can be averaged, or one round can be weighted more to arrive at the student's final score for the exam. We recommend trying this technique as practice before an actual exam. Viji often uses two-stage exams in her research methods course and loves the collaboration and ingenuity students exhibit to get to the correct answers. For example, her instructions are to use only the brainpower in the room (no outside searches or reviewing notes). One semester, someone creatively offered to lead a whole-class discussion. Together, students argued for different response options and, in most cases, landed on the correct answer. The energy in the room was unparalleled, and no doubt helped to solidify a collaborative rather than a competitive community of students.

- Can you offer students opportunities to explain questions that may seem ambiguous to them? If you decide that you need an in-person exam, could students write in a rationale for any questions they have? One way Kelly has implemented this is to add a concluding question: "Did any questions seem ambiguous to you, and why?" Doing so gives you some insight on why they may have provided a particular answer, as well as helping you refine the question for future use and grade fairly. Often, it is through this dialogue with students that we uncover cultural knowledge or vocabulary that may serve as a barrier to students answering correctly.

- Can you eliminate bias and jargon in your test-writing? No matter what format you choose, write questions well and avoid bias (Brame, n.d.; Sibley, 2014; Kansas State Department of Education, n.d.). Questions that rely on knowledge obtained outside the class will disadvantage students without that knowledge (such as idioms and sports references). Eliminate jargon in the test, particularly to reduce the cognitive load for multilingual learners. Always encourage students to ask you what a word means if they are unsure.

- Are you avoiding response options such as "all of the above" or "none of the above"? For multiple-choice questions, try avoiding too many questions that include an "all of the above" or "none of the above" option, as they tend to disadvantage weaker test-takers who may know the content, but aren't able to demonstrate it (Haladyna, Downing, & Rodriguez, 2002; Haladyna & Downing, 1989; DiBattista, Sinnige-Egger, & Fortuna, 2014).

- Can you incorporate elements that embrace diversity in your question-writing? For example, many of us like to refer to a named individual in a problem: "Ted has X . . ." Consider using names from minoritized groups. Similarly, you can cite the work of minoritized scholars in your test questions.

- Are you able to incorporate humor in your exam? There are studies that show that humor can dispel anxiety (Berk, 2000; Rodriguez & Albano, 2017) and inserting the occasional comic strip or humorous name or scenario can lighten the mood and put students at ease. If you are giving an exam online, incorporation of GIFs or memes are easy ways to do this.

What Can You Do Just Before an Exam to Foster Inclusion?

There are some things we can do ahead of an exam to add structure and transparency. Questions you might ask yourself include:

- Are you indicating the format and length of the exam? Recall that as an expert, you are likely to answer questions much more quickly than students. It might be tempting to force a number of questions per minute, but there are other factors to consider. Application and evaluation questions are more time-consuming than recall questions. Questions with long passages are more time-consuming than shorter ones. This can be particularly challenging to determine in your first time teaching a course. If the exam is lengthier than you had originally planned, you might try alternate scoring methods (see below). Perhaps you have colleagues or teaching assistants to weigh in on the length and complexity of the exam. If you can, release prior versions from a different semester. These practice exams can help ease anxiety for students.
- Can you email or post the directions ahead of time? In a rush to maximize time, students may not carefully attune to your test instructions. Sending the instructions portion of your assessment to students in the days before the exam helps orient them to the task.
- Are you letting them know that you want them to do well on the exam? There are many ways we can say or convey in a message that we, too, hope that they do well on an exam. Kelly has had students copy a sentence on the top of the exam

that says, "I can do this!" Viji tells her students: "These exams tell us as much about how well I have taught as they will tell you about what you have learned." This notion of shared success helps communicate that we are part of the same team working toward a common goal of understanding the material and gaining skills. These kinds of messages are a far cry from the classic statement, "look to your right, look to your left, one of you won't pass this class." However, if we don't state our hopes clearly, how will students know we feel this way?

What Can You Do During an Exam Session to Foster Inclusion?

The moments before an exam can be a stressful time for some students. This is also a prime opportunity for building community, showing that you care, and communicating your belief in your students' abilities.

- Can you put them at ease? Consider starting the class with a poll question where they can offer words of encouragement to their peers. This also builds community and a sense that their collective success is valued. You could show a fun video, a montage of photos like puppies, or anything that you feel might help them feel at ease. One semester, Viji recalls it was an unseasonably wet and icy day, so she dimmed the lights and projected a video of a fireplace on the front screen as students filed in. Kelly likes to make students laugh by having them watch silly videos she makes of herself. You could ask students to help compile a motivational playlist and play some of these songs at the beginning of your assessment sessions. All of these ideas help build community and a shared sense of success.
- Are you providing guidelines about what students can leave out or need to put away? Indicate how they may ask you a

question or request to leave the room if needed. We hear from students that they are not allowed to use the bathroom during some exams. Some students will need access to a bathroom because they are humans and they have bodily functions. Again, don't leave it to chance that some students will know what is appropriate to request during a testing session and others will not.

- Are you able to post the remaining time and exam clarifications visibly for all? Have a system, such as a white board or large screen, that broadcasts clarifications that might be helpful to the whole group during the testing session. Post the time or a countdown timer visibly for all to see. We find it helpful to provide a warning at key times (five minutes remain, one minute remains) to help students manage any final tasks they should complete. You can add statements in the exam to help students manage their time such as, "if you use about twenty minutes for the multiple-choice section, you will have forty minutes to complete the open-ended questions."

- Can you bring in some items that are likely to be used by students during the testing session? Bring a pencil sharpener, stapler, extra pencils, or any other materials that students may need but may have forgotten. Having cough drops and tissues for students who may need them is another thoughtful gesture. These are the little things that show you care for students.

What Can You Do After an Exam to Foster Inclusion?

Regardless of the format of your exams, you'll want to provide a timeline for when students might expect to see their scores. Of course, timely feedback is most appreciated, but is not always possible. Work to grade expediently, but thoughtfully.

- Are you grading with rubrics? As mentioned earlier, blind grading minimizes bias. Use rubrics for open-ended questions. If you have graders for the course, assign a grader to assess all of a single question or sets of questions for consistency.
- Are you adjusting your grading using your diagnostic data? Use data to determine the quality of a question. Depending on how the grading is done, you may be privy to some test analysis data. Often, these reports include terms such as item difficulty and item discrimination. If you are unfamiliar with these, there are likely individuals in your institution's teaching center who can help interpret them. In general, from a test construction standpoint, questions that nearly all or none of the students get right don't offer much information. Decide how to handle questions that very few answer correctly. You may opt to drop questions that don't meet a certain threshold, or to give back points. The latter doesn't penalize students who may have gotten that one correct but a different one wrong. One of the rationales for dropping questions or points is that it conveys to the students that it is OK that they collectively didn't understand a concept (or that your question was unclear). In these instances, we can say: "We're not where we need to be yet, but we'll work on it for the next assessment."
- Are you discussing the results of the exam with your students? Provide aggregate data or a distribution of grouped scores (e.g., 59% or below, 60–69, 70–79, etc.) to provide context for students on their performance. Post-exam periods can be opportunities to incorporate instructor talk and define and remind students what it means to have a growth mind-set. We need to remember that students with a low grade are at risk of simply giving up and dropping the class.

To counteract those feelings, we can use our experience to talk about the many students we have seen make gains over the semester and succeed as they learned how to learn in the course.

- Can students see their exams? We've known a few colleagues who have very strict rules around returning exams, sometimes not even letting students review their mistakes. The rules are sometimes intended to keep students from coming in to quibble over a point or two in the grading. While we know this is why some students want to review their exams, what if we assumed the best about students before we meet them? When students ask to see their mistakes, it is because they see the exam as a learning opportunity for future encounters with similar material. These are students who know improvement is possible. Kelly posts a key with detailed explanations to provide clarity to all, not just ones that can attend her office hours.

- Are you contacting individual students after the exam? Use the exam as an opportunity to invite students to meet with you. Viji likes to individually contact students who did poorly on the first exam to tell them that she believes they can be successful. She invites them to meet to discuss their approach for the exam and how they might prepare differently for the next exam. One semester, she had a student in this situation come in, convinced that she couldn't turn her grade around. When Viji reminded her that the cumulative final could replace her first exam grade if it was better, she decided to stay in the course and take advantage of resources she hadn't used prior to the first exam. The student finished with a top grade but most important, she built confidence in herself and her academic abilities.

- Can you use the time after an exam to help students improve metacognition and foster community? Consider the use of an exam wrapper to help students improve their metacognition. Exam wrappers are short surveys that ask students how they prepared for the exam, how that preparation worked for them, and how they might improve. By using an exam wrapper, you are encouraging students to take ownership of their learning, and the data will allow you to see if and how students are using your course resources and what you may need to add to shore up support. Lastly, brainstorm ways you can foster community in the exam debrief period. We enjoy contacting students who did very well on the exam and encouraging them to offer tips that worked for them via a shared document. This serves multiple purposes: it affirms the good work of the students who did well, it encourages them to help their peers, and when the document is shared with the class, all members of the course benefit from the tips provided. It demonstrates a commitment to their collective success and that helping each other to succeed is valued and supported.

How Can Commitment to Inclusion Guide Your Course Policies?

Even as experienced instructors, we continually face the challenge of how and when to set policies that might bring more structure. We often bounce thorny issues like these off each other, as we help each other prioritize inclusive practices. Although there are too many circumstances to explore here, we hope to lay out a few examples and the questions we ask ourselves as our inclusive practices evolve.

Example 1: The laptop ban
Many an instructor has toyed with a blanket policy of banning laptops during class sessions. We have seen them distract our students and envision that without them, students

might better listen or engage in our course work. We might argue that it is inclusive to disallow them, because it helps students engage better, especially those who cannot self-regulate, and there is evidence to support their negative effects in classrooms (May, 2017). On the other side, there are some students who require laptops for accommodations. Banning laptops reveals the students with accessibility needs (Pryal & Jack, 2017) and may disadvantage others who simply learn better because they use technology wisely.

As often happens, we find many of these arguments to be student deficit-based rather than acknowledging a course deficit. In other words, what is the professor doing while students are on social media and shopping? Is there enough structure? Are all students being asked to engage in practice and collaboration frequently enough to remove the temptation to zone out on the laptop? We keep our students very active during our class sessions and observer after observer has been surprised that even with hundreds of students, very few are off-task. We think about the tempo, as James Lang calls it, nicely making the analogy of teaching to an orchestral performance (Lang, 2021). We build laptop usage into the class norms and agreements in which students practice holding themselves accountable, but peers and instructors can nudge a student who is not abiding by the norms. Sharing relevant studies like one by Faria Sana and colleagues in 2013 can help students realize that being visibly distracted can distract their peers and hinder classmates' learning (Sana, Weston, & Cepeda, 2013). The appendix of Lang's book *Distracted: Why Students Can't Focus and What You Can Do About It,* provides a sample device policy that briefly shares research about device distraction. He also offers language about the goals of the class that require active engagement, "If you are focused on your device, instead of your work, you are depriving the entire class of your ideas and questions—both of which we all want to hear" (Lang, 2020). In short, we refrain from using a heavy hand toward laptops or cell phones in favor of building a lot of structured practice into our courses and helping our students learn why and how to regulate themselves.

Is there some middle ground? One strategy to consider is asking students to put laptops away or close them periodically when they seem less necessary, such as during a whole-class discussion (this assumes you can still provide accommodations for students that need them, such as a recording). Another middle ground strategy some instructors use involves placing students in zones within the physical space. For example, Lisa Oakes, a developmental psychologist at the University of California, Davis, says, "I have a small laptop zone in my class; everyone else uses pen and paper or tablet and stylus. Students not on keyboards are much more engaged, participate more. However, I post podcast of lecture to allow them to fill in the gaps and to reduce anxiety" (Oakes, 2019). No matter what route we choose, we can acknowledge that staying focused is a challenge for all of us (instructors included). We should continue to reflect on the issue of laptops and inclusiveness.

Example 2: Turning cameras on for online meetings
As we all grappled with the sudden shift to remote instruction when COVID-19 hit, many instructors grew frustrated with the number of students who participated in Zoom classes with their cameras turned off. Naturally, it is easier to have a discussion when we can see one another. Some feared that students with cameras off weren't paying

attention and thus were not learning. As with the laptop ban, it seemed necessary to some educators to enforce a cameras-on requirement. Meanwhile, other instructors felt a camera requirement was not inclusive and not necessary. Karen Costa summarized her thoughts this way:

> "Requiring students to be on camera is contrary to everything we know about universal design for learning, about inclusive and trauma-aware teaching practices, and about making effective use of the affordances of online learning. We live in the most interesting times, in a global pandemic, and it's really not time to equivocate. Let me use my precious time with you wisely and say quickly and clearly that forcing students to be on camera is a terrible, horrible, no good, very bad policy" (Costa, 2020).

There are many reasons why a student may opt not to turn on their camera. In spring 2020 when we all shifted to online, none of us were prepared for how our private spaces suddenly became the backdrop for online classes or how it would feel to stare at ourselves on camera all day. Some students found that they didn't have the bandwidth to support the technology with the camera. And others were tasked with new responsibilities while taking their own classes, such as caretaking.

We approached the decision-making much like the laptop ban, as we learned from other educators who were feeling similarly. We tried to make student-centered decisions. We thought about why many instructors wanted the camera on—to be able to monitor student attention and to make talking at a screen less uncomfortable. We wanted to assess engagement through more objective measures. After all, a daydreamer could still nod and appear to be attentive. We settled on some ideas that helped us with the great camera debate of 2020:

- We monitored engagement with frequent, formative assessment questions, such as polls, shared documents, and asking students to type in the chat.
- We worked with students to create a shared classroom code of conduct, which included a discussion about why it is helpful and when it is helpful to have cameras to foster community and ownership in the class.
- We encouraged, but did not require, students to use cameras when they were in small breakout rooms with one another.
- We asked students to post profile pictures, so that even when their camera was not on, we would still have a representation of them.
- If we were going to be talking a lot or were asking the students to do independent work, we specifically prompted them to "feel free to turn your camera off during this time, as there is no benefit for community building during this activity."

By implementing these ideas, we became more comfortable and creative with the ways we gauged engagement and understanding. We found that there were plenty of students who used their cameras because they valued the community aspect too.

Example 3: I am so close to a [fill in the blank] grade. Can I please do some extra credit or turn in an assignment I missed?
We have yet to meet a single instructor who hasn't faced a question like this at the end of a semester. It can be exhausting to field a number of these requests. Keeping inclusion in mind, you might ask yourself the questions Kelly asks herself in a situation like this: "Would I do this for another student

with X case?" At times, the case is unusual and being flexible or accommodating is not at all unreasonable. In this situation, Viji asks herself: "How do I know if another student is experiencing something similar? Or who feels like they can ask and who doesn't?" This is a hard question to wrestle with. Some of our students would not ask for the rules to be applied differently to them, and so by refusing the ones who ask, we signal we are being fair. A different take is to build in what Nilson refers to in her book *Specifications Grading: Restoring Rigor, Motivating Students, and Saving Faculty Time* as "oops tokens" (Nilson, 2015). These are tokens that students can use at any time to turn in an assignment late or redo an assignment. No explanation is needed. Consider ways you can allow flexibility like this for your students so that all of them feel there is room for the rules to be bent, but in a way that is equitable.

In short, when it comes to rules and policies, ask yourself the following:

- Can students work as a group to establish norms that are best for learning, such that you are merely helping to enforce their preferences throughout the term?
- Can you bake in opportunities for flexibility that convey that life doesn't stop at the classroom doors and you are willing to accommodate requests equitably?
- For every policy or decision you make, who might be excluded because they did not think to ask about it or they did not know the unwritten rules?

How Do You Prepare an Instructional Team for Inclusiveness?

Many educators teach a class alone, but some have a co-instructor, graders, or undergraduate or graduate teaching assistants (TAs). Your efforts setting up a more inclusive course are at risk if you do not have buy-in or provide guidance to an instructional team to do the same. You'll want to prepare team members for your approach.

Provide some guidance about your expectations and common questions your course collaborators may have. Clear expectations can reveal your philosophy of teaching for novice instructors. For example, Viji prepared a handbook for TAs that includes answers to common logistical questions plus guidance on many of the topics outlined in this chapter, such as holding more inclusive office hours and approaches to grading equitably. You may also wish to assign readings or videos on inclusive teaching to help them grow as instructors.

Often, teaching in our courses may be a TAs first opportunity to learn about pedagogy. You won't be able to fit in all the lessons of good teaching along with their other responsibilities, so instead pay close attention to your introduction and framing of the course and keep an agenda of times throughout the course that you can discuss different issues in teaching before they arise—a just-in-time approach to instruction. Hold regular discussions with the team, perhaps brainstorming solutions to common scenarios or role-playing student interactions. This will bring transparency to your instructional choices and help keep open lines of communication among the team. Members of the team should feel comfortable approaching you about policies and procedures and to establish shared goals. When these practices are done well, the team will feel the same sense of ownership that students in the course have, will learn about teaching, and will have ideas about how to make their own teaching more inclusive.

INSTRUCTOR CHECKLIST

Tips for communicating inclusion via email:

- Use the student's name exactly as it is spelled.
- Model inclusive language by including a pronoun and/or name pronunciation guide after your signature.
- Aim for a warm tone and never shame a student.
- Pay attention and email students to let them know you notice their good efforts or that you are concerned about their absences.

Bringing transparency and inclusion to office hours:

- Demystify office hours by telling your students what they are for and how they can meet with you.
- Create formats and options for students that vary the location, time, and nature of the meetings to allow a variety of students to visit.
- Use a sign-up tool to add transparency about your availability and confirm that the student will be able to meet with you for their assigned time.
- If holding office hours in your own office, think about how that space is perceived by students and make it as welcoming and nonthreatening as possible.

- Use your office hours to make meaningful connections with students to learn about their lives and interests and how you can support them in their pursuits.

Creating inclusive assignments:

- Use assignments to work in ideas and topics that are of interest to students in your course or campus, especially as they pertain to diversity, equity, and inclusion.
- Offer students some autonomy in what they chose to do for assignments, to allow them to link your content to their interests.
- Grade assignments blindly and with a rubric to minimize bias in evaluation.
- Provide feedback in a timely manner with a helpful tone.

Creating inclusive exams:

- Set the stage for success in your exams by focusing on frequent formative feedback that aligns in content, difficulty, and format with your summative assessments.
- Provide transparency of exam-caliber questions in practice assignments by labeling them as typical test questions (TTQs).
- Share old exams, instructions for the exam, and as much information as possible about the structure of the exam ahead of the testing session.
- If a study guide or prior exam is useful to prepare students for the exam, require students to complete it by making it an assignment.
- Take care to write clear and unbiased exam questions.

- During an exam session, cultivate a supportive community by creating a welcoming environment in which you ask students to encourage each other through a class poll, where you provide encouragement and a sincere wish for their success and bring some helpful supplies that convey that you care.
- Encourage transparency about the rules during the exam, including how to ask questions, if they are permitted to visit the restroom, where they will see updates or clarifications to exam questions, and time remaining in the testing session.
- After an exam, consider the results carefully, make any necessary adjustments to scoring, and debrief students about their performance.
- Encourage students who did well to contribute to their peers' preparation for the next exam, and students who did poorly to visit with you to work together to identify a plan to improve.
- Incorporate exam wrappers to enhance metacognition and help you identify resources needed by students.

Decision-making:

- Use an inclusive lens when asked to alter your policies: "Would I be willing to offer this accommodation to another student who asks?"
- Rather than relying on individual students to ask for accommodations, consider ways to provide these to all. One example is the idea of "oops tokens" which allow students to miss an assignment or turn it in late without having to disclose the reason.

- Bring students into the discussion of topics like laptops in the classroom or keeping cameras on in online meetings, so that you can work together to develop a shared code of conduct rather than enforce these policies with a heavy hand.

Preparing an instructional team:

- Provide guidelines and structure to an instructional team to help them understand your goals and teaching philosophy in action.
- Have routine discussions with the team that bring transparency to your decisions and allow them to learn to be inclusive in their teaching approach in the future.

CHAPTER 7

REFLECTING AND DOCUMENTING YOUR INCLUSIVE PRACTICES

Suppose you are up for a promotion in your department. In your teaching statement, you write "I create an inclusive classroom environment" without much discussion about what this means and how an evaluator can verify the declaration. While we trust readers of our book wouldn't throw these words around, if we were considering this statement we would ask, "What pieces of evidence in the dossier demonstrate that an inclusive classroom environment is created?"

In this chapter, we will dive into ways to reflect on and revise your inclusive strategies to make them visible to others. As you become more comfortable with defining and identifying inclusive teaching, we hope you can become a change agent in your own spaces and institutions, helping others define and reward it during decisions about hiring, reappointment, tenure, promotion, teaching, awards and more.

Are You Self-Reflecting and Demonstrating Change and Growth?

In developing teaching expertise, there is no single start line and no single finish line. We want to encourage you to simply start where you are. Begin reflecting on what you are learning about inclusive teaching and how you are putting it into practice. You will make some mistakes, some that you'll see right away and others that you will decide were mistakes many semesters later. As you do this kind of work, your students are the winners. Beyond focusing on the benefits for students, this kind of reflection often provides evidence that can be used in your own teaching dossier, typically in the form of a teaching philosophy or diversity statement.

You may want to employ daily reflections, which can be helpful for thinking about the small details you might otherwise overlook when you think about teaching over the course of a semester. Perhaps you have a journal or some other system that you can use to reflect about what went well or didn't go well after each class. Viji squeezes this in as she walks out of the classroom, recording voice memo notes to herself. Kelly often carries her syllabus or course schedule in her bag and scribbles notes next to each day. These kinds of quick reflections must become habits. As people who struggle to exercise every day, we know it can be hard to form good habits. Even if you miss a few days, something is better than nothing.

Perhaps the most informative suggestion (and one that we know many readers will cringe at) is to record yourself during one or several class sessions throughout the term. Then you can watch or listen to your teaching, observing yourself through the lens of inclusivity. Audio and visual are both informative, alone or combined, as you watch yourself teach. The audio file can also be useful if you want to have it analyzed for sound. We're certain this will become more commonplace. As of this writing, we're aware of one free tool called Decibel Analysis for Research in Teaching (DART) that can distinguish among silence, a single voice, and multiple voices talking at the same time (Owens et al., 2017). This kind of sound analysis can give an instructor a quick snapshot of how much time they are giving students time to silently think during a think-pair-share or what percent of the class time is devoted to small-group discussion. Fast Company describes an app called GenderEQ that categorizes male and female voices and provide the percentage of time each group spends talking in real time (Miller, 2017). This kind of tool could help an instructor determine if their classes have an inequity in participation by assumed gender. We're excited to see what is on the horizon with more tools like these that help us objectively evaluate aspects of our teaching.

As you've probably surmised, our favorite word is *structure,* and we have some ideas about implementing reflections that are more structured. Because there is so much to reflect upon after each class, we want to encourage you to be intentional about inclusivity, in addition to anything else you want to record. We'll get you started with a few daily prompts, but you should feel free to edit these to suit your own needs. Change them as you grow each semester:

- In what ways did I receive contributions from all students, not just the volunteers willing to speak up?
- How regularly did I use non-content instructor talk to help students feel a sense of belonging in our learning community or emphasize how important a growth mind-set is for learning?

- Did the course materials I assigned for out of class help me bring low-stakes practice to the class session?
- How often did I make meaningful connections with individual students?
- Are there any students I'm concerned about that I should check in on?
- How do I know all students are learning today?
- What didn't go well and why? What did go well? What can I try next time?

We are often not our best judges, so beyond your own daily reflections you will need others' viewpoints too. These perspectives can come from students and peers. Let's explore how outside feedback can inform your own journey to more inclusive teaching.

How Can Students Inform Your Growth?

Students are not receptacles of knowledge; they are our partners in the learning and in our development as teachers. We can learn much from students when we listen and ask the right questions.

How Can We Gather Informal Micro-Feedback?
We are often less effective at capturing the small details if we reflect only at the end of each semester or only when we're asked to write a teaching philosophy. Similarly, student voices and suggestions can be very powerful and specific when shared with us more frequently than just at the end of the semester. We can hear their voices in small and routine ways. We like to think of this as micro-feedback. To illustrate our ideas, here are a few concrete examples to capture micro-feedback:

Poll: Ask students, "How long did the reading assignment take last night"? Students can respond with concrete numbers because they just completed this, and you can see the range of answers to inform your course design. If your reading assignments are taking students longer than you anticipated, who is this hurting the most? You may also be able to identify individual students who are taking much more time than their peers. Consider offering to meet with these students to discuss and, possibly, intervene with strategies for success.

Thumbs up/thumbs down: Tell students, "Before we end today, discretely give me a thumbs up if you found something in our discussion that related to your own life or a thumbs down if not so much." While there won't be total agreement from students, use this to gauge if you've hit your mark with content relevance for most students. Additionally, this can be used to open a conversation with their ideas.

Question at the end of a collaborative assignment: ask students, "Did you feel included in your group; why or why not?" (Remind students, "Responses are just for me; they will not be shared with peers.") Questions like this help an instructor to assess how collaboration is going, with an opportunity to intervene or provide better guidelines to the whole class before the next collaborative assignment. In a large class, you may not be able to give attention to every student but skimming the responses and giving a summary to students will still make them feel visible and acknowledged.

Continuous open anonymous survey: instruct students, "Please use this survey link to comment about any aspects of the course that are going well for you or could be changed to improve your learning." If this form is visible in multiple places and referenced in class, students can let an instructor know at any time, even in the middle of a class session, what is working or not working for them. The instructor can set up the survey so that they get an email alert when a response is received. Kelly makes this survey link visible on her syllabus, on the front page of her learning management system, and in her weekly emails to students. There are dangers with complete anonymity but having this as a mechanism can be invaluable for a student who is feeling unsure about sharing thoughts with you any other way. An instructor can't intervene with a particular student if they decide to remain anonymous on this form, but the instructor may be able to make changes or discuss the issue with the whole class.

By collecting micro-feedback, we are routinely signaling to students the value we place on being inclusive and the partnership they bring to the course. In this spirit, we should aim to make at least one change (if not more) during the semester to show students we are willing to respond to feedback midstream.

How Can You Best Use Formal Feedback Mechanisms?
The four examples above are helpful for informal feedback that you can implement on the fly throughout the semester. There are other, more formal forms of feedback from students that are often used at specific points in the semester. More formal feedback often includes midsemester evaluations and end-of-course evaluations. Most units and institutions don't have formal midsemester evaluations or even require them. Thus, midsemester feedback offers a useful personalized learning opportunity for instructors. End-of-course evaluations are typically standardized, and often allow for instructor-added questions too. Of course, you can't learn much if only 10–15 percent of your students complete these surveys, and such a small percentage may not

be representative of your class. To improve response rates, we recommend providing class time to work on the surveys and perhaps offering an incentive. Some educators give individual participation points or extra credit, while others give the entire class extra credit if the completion rate is over some threshold (i.e., 90 percent of the class or higher).

What questions should you ask related to inclusion on a midsemester or end-of-course evaluation? Some questions that have prompted rich student answers include:

- In what ways has your instructor demonstrated they care about your learning?
- Is there content from the assignments or class discussions that has made you feel included or excluded? Explain.
- How did the diversity of your classmates contribute to your learning in this course?
- How might the class climate be made more inclusive?

Besides appearing on surveys, these questions are great to ask to students in a focus group setting. In focus groups, students have a conversation leading to ideas that become better developed and often becomes suggestions. As an example, we moderated a public forum discussion about inclusive classrooms with students at our institution. The discussion evolved and some students said that they were tired of being left out of think-pair-shares if they weren't sitting with someone they knew. Kelly used this specific feedback to be more mindful about assigning discussion groups and not leaving to chance that all learners would find a partner or two. She shared this with colleagues, and as a result some other instructors in the department also began assigning discussion groups. While you can hold a focus group with your current or past students, it can be beneficial to find a colleague willing to do this for you. Often, this is the kind of facilitator role someone from a teaching and learning center can play. The facilitator then gives you a summary of the conversation. This way, students are free of the power you hold as someone grading them or writing a future letter of recommendation and can feel more open to providing candid feedback.

Do You Curate Unsolicited Feedback?

Some of the best feedback we've received from students about our inclusive strategies has been unsolicited. For example, Kelly often sends an email to students in her very large biology class if she sees large gains in their exam scores. She lets them know she sees the good work they are doing, regardless of the grades they are receiving. Students reply with responses that inform her teaching and her advice to future students. The end of the semester is often a time when students send unsolicited praise too.

Viji has a folder in her inbox with these kinds of unsolicited messages, and she has encouraged many other colleagues to systematically store them. These messages are both useful in a dossier and for a day when you need an emotional boost. Most of the unsolicited feedback we've both received has been positive. It's important to underscore that students with less positive experiences will also need an outlet to share their thoughts around inclusion—thus the more structured polls, assignments, and surveys we've discussed.

Do You Capitalize on Reflection and Feedback on the Last Day of Class?

Before we move away from discussing student feedback, let's take a moment to think about the quality of student feedback. If our questions are well-structured, we should get the information we are seeking that informs our own learning. However, when do we teach students to give quality feedback? While we can do this any time in the semester, we've found the last week or last day of class (LDOC) is an effective time to reinforce reflection and feedback for their own learning. In turn, it improves the responses we get on end of semester evaluations. Our discussions with students on LDOC prime them to give us the kind of quality feedback we seek. Below are a few recommendations for LDOC based on our years of teaching:

- Don't focus only on content and finishing material. If you find you always need this last day to finish regular business, rethink your schedule and content so that you have more time to facilitate reflection.
- Do focus on growth and learning beyond the grade. Kelly's husband is a chemistry professor, and when he teaches general chemistry he is not shy about telling his students that he got a C in both semesters of general chemistry. He uses this to help students see that even final grades don't define destiny. However, there is immense privilege in being able to self-disclose shortcomings like these, which can have negative consequences for women, people of color, and other groups. Students may use these disclosures against instructors because of implicit biases (Kreitzer & Sweet-Cushman, 2021).

- Continue to invite students into your discipline, either formally or informally. Viji knows that most students who fear her statistics course have a fixed mind-set that "they are just not a math person." By the end of the semester, she has plenty of examples to illustrate how her students can spot a terrible infographic on news websites or how data can be used to support an argument. She makes sure students reflect on how they are using math in their everyday life, and she hopes that they won't stop there. She shows students that they are all "math people" who can formally continue in her upper-level statistics course or informally continue to see the value of math in everyday life.
- Revisit the learning goals for the course and let students reflect on all the work and collaborative learning they did to get to LDOC. Link these goals to skills students are interested in for their future careers. For example, Kelly shares with her introductory biology students this sentiment around assigned discussion groups: "When I asked you to talk to your group to explain your thoughts or convince them you were right, you practiced your communication skills, you practiced persuading someone your ideas had merit, you practiced listening to others with different ideas and perspectives, you practiced teaching your peers, and you practiced cooperation, kindness, and overall collaboration. I'm proud of you and you should be proud of that too."
- Remind students that they are partners in your own learning and that you value their constructive feedback. Many students don't know that instructors read their own evaluations—they are under the impression these are some kind of letters to the administration. Let students know you read all their evaluations and how they can best provide feedback. We like to employ analogies. We have them envision us providing feedback on one of their essays with "good job" or "needs work" or "I love your shoes." These comments wouldn't be

very useful for becoming a better writer or thinker. Thus, we provide examples of feedback that are helpful and show them why they are helpful, such as "I appreciated all of the resources that were available" or "I really liked that the review sessions were recorded because I couldn't attend" or "The exams were hard, but I felt prepared."

- Help students connect the academic skills they used with professional skills they can add to a résumé to gain valuable opportunities. A campus career service representative might be interested in talking with students about this.
- Ask students to reflect by writing an advice note to future students of the course. These can be brought into the next term's syllabus or class site, building community across terms.

With activities designed to reflect on the semester, especially on learning outcomes and sense of belonging, students will be better primed to see the value of end-of-course surveys (that hopefully we should have saved class time for). Students will begin to see the surveys as a rewarding reflection activity for their own growth.

How Can Peers Inform Your Growth?

Students can provide feedback based on their own experiences. However, colleagues can provide a different perspective, which can be more objective. Not all instructors have experience with objective feedback because many peer observations are not completed with rubrics that help to mitigate personal bias. Additionally, many instructors have received only feedback that is required and is often associated with a high-stakes review processes for employment. To grow and learn, educators need what their students need—low-stakes practice and feedback.

Who can help you learn and grow as an instructor in this way? We hope you can find many people who do this for you, as we have. We even met and began our professional relationship and personal friendship through this process. We were in a faculty learning community together, assigned to small groups to do peer observations. Not surprisingly, we were both working on strategies to be more inclusive of more students in our teaching. After observing each other, we had plenty to talk about over coffee—for years and years.

It's worth pointing out that we are not in the same disciplines, so when we watch each other teach we don't get bogged down in disciplinary content. We more easily shift our attention away from ourselves and toward the teaching strategies we are observing. For example, "Is that how I would have explained that concept?" becomes "She explained some concept called X, but all the students did not have a chance to practice it. Is this concept difficult or important enough that it warrants class time for all students to practice?" When you want feedback on your content and level of difficulty, by all means seek out people in your discipline. When you want someone to provide feedback about inclusive participation strategies or your use of non-content instructor talk, you may want to connect to colleagues through a teaching and learning center. The additional benefit is that people outside your discipline likely won't be evaluating you in future high-stakes employment decisions. You can let your defenses down and learn more.

As practitioners who both give and receive peer reviews regularly, we have some advice for conducting a formative peer observation. First, do not limit it to what can be observed in the classroom environment. As observers, we appreciate seeing the fuller picture with a syllabus, access to the learning management system, and anything else the instructor thinks is a major component of the course design. These extras give us context for what we are seeing in one session (in what we've heard others call "drive-by observations"). Second, we think it's best to schedule a quick coffee or chat before and after the classroom observation to learn what the instructor hopes to get from the observation and to make sure written words are not misunderstood. Being observed and critiqued requires a teacher to be vulnerable, so it's best to take care in crafting the words and considering how they will be received. Third, we recommend experimenting with rubrics that an observer can use, in addition to other comments they may have. Rubrics help measure distinct aspects of teaching, and help the observer focus on objective ideas rather than their opinion of what effective teaching may look like. Kelly wished her very first observer had a rubric, since he would have been less likely to comment about the noise of her heels as she walked around the room.

What rubrics or measurement instruments do we recommend using in formative peer observations and reviews? Different instruments measure different aspects of teaching. No one instrument can do everything.

As an example, when we want to know the percentage of class time we are devoting to small-group discussions and classroom response system polls (we are all inherently terrible at estimating this) we need a tool that can code activities over time. With the Classroom Observation Protocol for Undergraduate STEM (COPUS) tool, the observer records what is happening in two-minute intervals, by checking off what the instructor is doing and what students are doing from a list of codes. See table 7.1 for the list of codes (Smith et al,. 2013). COPUS requires little training to use, and there is an app-based version developed at UC Davis called the Generalized Observation and Reflection Platform (GORP). If

Table 7.1 Classroom Observation Protocol for Undergraduate STEM (COPUS) codes

1. Students Are Doing

L	Listening to instructor/taking notes, etc.
Ind	Individual thinking/problem solving. Only mark when an instructor explicitly asks students to think about a clicker question or another question/problem on their own.
CG	Discuss clicker question in groups of 2 or more students
WG	Working in groups on worksheet activity
OG	Other assigned group activity, such as responding to instructor question
AnQ	Student answering a question posed by the instructor with rest of class listening
SQ	Student asks question
WC	Engaged in whole class discussion by offering explanations, opinion, judgment, etc. to whole class, often facilitated by instructor
Prd	Making a prediction about the outcome of demo or experiment
SP	Presentation by student(s)
TQ	Test or quiz
W	Waiting (instructor late, working on fixing AV problems, instructor otherwise occupied, etc.)
O	Other: explain in comments

2. Instructor Is Doing

Lec	Lecturing (presenting content, deriving mathematical results, presenting a problem solution, etc.)
RtW	Real-time writing on board, doc, projector (often checked off along with Lec)
FUp	Follow-up/feedback on clicker question or activity to entire class
PQ	Posing non-clicker question to students (non-rhetorical)
CQ	Asking a clicker question (mark the entire time the instructor is using a clicker question, not just when first asked)
AnQ	Listening to and answering student questions with entire class listening
MG	Moving through class guiding ongoing student work during active learning task
1o1	One-on-one extended discussion with one or a few individuals, not paying attention to the rest of the class (can be along with MG or AnQ)
D/V	Showing or conducting a demo, experiment, simulation, video, or animation
Adm	Administration (assign homework, return tests, etc.)
W	Waiting when there is an opportunity for an instructor to be interacting with or observing/listening to student or group activities and the instructor is not doing so
O	Other: explain in comments

Source: Reproduced by permission from Smith et al. 2013.

our goal is to build community and let students practice their learning, then knowing how we use our time (talking versus student time practicing and collaborating) is an important metric in our inclusive teaching reflections. From these more objective measures, we can determine if this is where we want to be or if we need to find ways to deliver some of our talking points outside of class time.

If we want to know how our non-content instructor talk is being used, we will need a different tool. Kimberly Tanner's research group has done an initial characterization and coding of instructor talk that can be a useful tool for formative evaluation, if we follow the categories (see examples in each category) (Seidel et al., 2015). In table 7.2, we provide the research group's categories. While the last category relates to science, another disciplinary context can be substituted.

Remember, it's not just our classroom experiences that can be open for review. For example, if we want to know if our syllabus projects an inclusive tone and illustrates inclusive course design, then we'll want to turn to a syllabus rubric. We've identified some that are labeled learner-centered, and these often intersect with many of the points we've made throughout the book. Looking over these rubrics can be informative. For example, one from the University of Virginia's Center for Teaching Excellence has categories to be checked such as:

- "Syllabus clearly communicates high expectations and projects confidence that students can meet them through hard work."
- "There is evidence of plans for frequent formative assessments with immediate feedback from a variety of sources (e.g., self, peer, instructor, computer generated, community). These low-stakes, formative assessments allow students to 'practice' before high-stakes summative assessments."

Table 7.2   Types of non-content instructor talk

Category	Subcategories	Example Statements
Building the Instructor/Student Relationship	1. Demonstrating Respect for Students 2. Revealing Secrets to Success 3. Boosting Self-Efficacy	*Boosting self-efficacy:* "I'm not putting it up there because I'm disappointed in you. A lot of smart people that I know, including faculty members that I know, have a hard time with this material, okay. So, I know that you can do it."
Establishing Classroom Culture	1. Pre-framing Classroom Activities 2. Practicing Scientific Habits of Mind 3. Building a Biology Community among Students 4. Giving Credit to Colleagues 5. Indicating That It Is Okay to Be Wrong or Disagree	*Building a community:* "Raise your hand if you need an index card. People around you are with you and they will share. Somebody pass an index card to those people."
Explaining Pedagogical Choices	• Supporting Learning through Teaching Choices • Using Student Work to Drive Teaching Choices • Connecting Biology to the Real World and Career • Discussing How People Learn • Fostering Learning for the Long Term	*Fostering learning for the long term:* "The reason I have you guys interact is because when you interact with each other, the learning that takes place, you'll retain that a lot longer than if I just tell you the answer. You learn stuff by explaining it to somebody and by hearing your own colleagues tell you about it."
Sharing Personal Experiences	• Recounting Personal Information/Anecdotes • Relating to Student Experiences	*Recounting personal information:* "I was born and raised in [city, state], very far away from here. I'm first-generation college-going. My dad is first-generation graduating from high school, something that's a point of pride in my family."

Table 7.2   Types of non-content instructor talk

Category	Subcategories	Example Statements
Unmasking Science	• Being Explicit about the Nature of Science • Promoting Diversity in Science	*Promoting Diversity:* "We absolutely know, we have lots of stories that say the kinds of people who do science affect the kinds of questions that get asked, affect the kinds of data that gets acknowledged, and the kind of data that gets ignored. So, that's why it's really important to have a diverse group of people doing science."

Source: Reproduced by permission from Seidel et al. 2015.

These tools for evaluating student/instructor behaviors, instructor talk, and syllabi are just a few ways to achieve this kind of objective peer review. In the next few years, we predict we will see more and more rubrics and apps developed that call our attention to issues of diversity and inclusion in course materials, course design, and student-instructor interactions.

What Data Can Inform Your Growth?

We are living in an increasingly data-driven world. No matter what your discipline, data that you can generate or obtain can inform your inclusive teaching strategies. We'll be brief in this section, because the kinds of data you can generate and obtain will be context-dependent by discipline and institution. We'll expand on what we mean with a few examples, knowing that learning analytics is a fast-expanding field.

Data that you can generate with your students can include survey questions that get at perceptions, behaviors, or knowledge. These may be useful as single questions at the end of a course but it can be powerful to ask the same questions, or highly similar parallel questions, at both the beginning and the end of the semester. You can look at class averages and individual changes for each question. Staff at centers for teaching and learning can help instructors design these kinds of surveys. Such data are useful for measuring learning gains, but let's look at a few sample questions that could transcend any discipline and relate to inclusive teaching strategies.

- Perception: *"People who are good at a particular skill were born with a higher level of natural ability."* (Students indicate a level of agreement with this statement.) This is one of many questions related to a student's growth versus fixed mind-set, as described by Carol Dweck (Dweck, 2006). You may choose to use a validated range of mind-set questions if you want to more deeply explore the effect of your course on mind-set (Dweck, 1999).
- Behavior: *"I often participate in class discussions."* (Students indicate a level of agreement with this statement.) A question like this can help you see if you are using small-group discussions enough for most students to feel included.
- Knowledge related to diversity: *"Please share as many examples as you can of how women, Black, Indigenous, or people of color contributed to the field we are studying."* A question along these lines helps you see how well you are doing bringing a diverse set of scholars into your course.

There are likely other data you are collecting in your teaching that require no extra planning. For instance, if students are working on a skill such as writing, then you'll have examples of student writing from the beginning and end of the semester. You can look for evidence of learning for all students, and you may want to consider how your strategies helped a particular type of student (e.g., multilingual). If you are using a classroom response system, you likely have data on questions you asked students to answer alone and again after a peer discussion. Do these associated data support the collaborative learning environment you are trying to create?

You may need help gathering other kinds of data, like student demographics and grades linked to demographics. You may find it necessary to discuss with your administrators how you can obtain these kinds of data. What can you learn from these data? If you wanted to know which students are transfers, you can simply ask them to self-identify and they likely will. Perhaps you want to know what percentage of your students are of lower socioeconomic status. You can't ask a question like this to students in your own survey, but institutions can probably supply you with these de-identified data after the semester ends. Knowing the demographics of your institution and your own students is useful for connecting with them. When one of our colleagues saw the demographics of his first-year course, he decided the reading list was not the best fit and immediately made changes. Knowing if there are performance disparities with your students based on demographics are also impactful data. While you may make rough assumptions around some characteristics such as student gender, it will be much harder to surmise if you have gaps between first-generation and non–first-generation college students.

Demographic data can be difficult to obtain from institutional offices. They are kept highly secure, for good reason. We have been fortunate at our university to help develop a dashboard for all instructors to examine these kinds of data after each semester (University Gazette, 2019). A dashboard eliminates a need to submit individual requests for each kind of report an instructor may want to access. Knowing colleagues at other universities that have also developed data analytics dashboards, we're certain these tools will become more prevalent throughout higher education in the next few years.

How Can You Demonstrate Your Commitment to Inclusive Teaching in a Dossier?

Until now, we've framed all the reflection and growth to benefit your learning and improvement as an educator. However, these activities (such as writing reflections, having peers observe you, collecting data) can serve double duty as evidence in a dossier for a new position, reappointment, promotion, or tenure. We've been saddened to see on our own campus how little evidence is included in dossiers about teaching, let alone evidence demonstrating a commitment to diversity, inclusion, and equity in teaching. For example, some teaching statements aren't much more than a description of courses taught. We rarely see syllabi in the dossier, which would be helpful as evidence of one's philosophy translated into action. Because we care deeply about this topic and have opportunities as campus administrators to influence changes, we have thought a great deal about what evidence of effective teaching looks like and what evidence of a commitment to inclusive teaching might look like.

We've also learned much from collaborations with other universities where teachers are working hard to define this. One framework we and other campuses have adapted is the Teaching Evaluation (TEval) rubric created as a collaboration between the University of Massachusetts, University of Kansas, University of Colorado at Boulder, and Michigan

State University (Weaver et al.. 2020). We've observed Andrea Greenhoot, one of the developers of the TEval rubric, discuss teaching evaluation at workshops. She often asks faculty to make a list of all the ways they spend their time on teaching-related activities outside the classroom. Through this exercise, we've witnessed participants quickly grasp the need for better rubrics describing much more than the time we spend with students. The TEval framework has seven dimensions, with optional levels indicating if someone is developing, proficient, or an expert in each dimension. The seven dimensions are listed below (with various subdimensions not shown):

1. Goals, content, and alignment
2. Teaching practices
3. Achievement of learning outcomes
4. Classroom culture and student perceptions
5. Mentoring and advising
6. Reflection and iterative growth
7. Involvement in teaching service, scholarship, or community

Importantly, the rubric asks for at least two pieces of evidence for each dimension. It's useful to evaluate the evidence you might already be developing and gathering if you are a self-reflective teacher with a commitment to inclusive teaching.

As an example, let's consider the sixth dimension: reflection and iterative growth. Your teaching philosophy centered on diversity, inclusion, and equity would be a piece of evidence to use here. This dimension is not about being perfect, so show how you've come to learn through your own reflection, student feedback, and peer feedback. Other pieces of evidence could be student comments that were impactful in your changes, syllabi from two different semesters that show how you changed their tone, or ways you've adjusted low-stakes practice for all students. These are just a few of many ways you could provide evidence of your reflection and continual development around inclusive teaching. Putting together a list of pieces of evidence that you might want to include in a future dossier is an effective way to wrap up your learning from this book.

We will get you started below with a list of pieces of evidence you could use to demonstrate a commitment to inclusive teaching. This is not an exhaustive list. We hope you will personalize it and create a dossier in which all the materials align with your teaching philosophy statement. You may need a table of contents and a descriptor about why you've included each document. This list is a summary of many topics we've discussed throughout the book, because a commitment to diversity, inclusion, and equity should permeate all aspects of your course and teaching. By creating a dossier that highlights your good work, you are helping to educate your colleagues who are reading these materials. We call that being a sneaky change agent!

COMPONENTS OF A DOSSIER DEMONSTRATING A COMMITMENT TO INCLUSIVE TEACHING AND LEARNING

Reflective statements (separate or combined in one document):

- A teaching philosophy statement that aligns with and helps explain why you've included the other documents. For example, if you discuss your reasoning for

intentionally using clear expectations and visual instructions to help all learners engage in structured active
learning, then point to a few places in the dossier where
the reader can find an example of this (e.g., class slide or
a student quote).

- A diversity statement that highlights how as an educator you've come to understand diversity and systemic
barriers, and your past efforts and future goals related
to diversity, inclusion, and equity in higher education.

- A service statement that highlights the kind of service
you do to promote diversity, inclusion, and equity in
education. While a reader likely has a CV that includes
service, this statement aligns the service with a commitment to inclusion.

- A mentoring and advising statement. How does your understanding of inclusive teaching affect your work with
students one-on-one?

*Evidence of inclusive high structure, active learning course
design elements, and a commitment to content that focuses
on human diversity, inclusion, and equity issues:*

- Syllabi
- Sample assignments (homework, projects, and papers)
- Sample assessments (tests, quizzes, poll questions, other)
- Sample class slides
- Audiovisual clips of exemplary teaching moments

Evidence of gains for learning outcomes such as
content that highlights human diversity, inclusion,
and equity, as well as psychosocial factors that help
all students thrive (belonging, growth mind-set, value,
and motivation):

- Exemplary student work
- Learning gains (pre- and post- data, classroom response data, examples of student work at different points in the semester)
- Changes in perception and behaviors
- Student comments from emails or surveys
- Peer observation rubrics and quotes
- Data across terms that demonstrate growth or improvement

Evidence of the inclusive environment you foster for learning:

- Student comments from emails or surveys that can be grouped for themes such as building confidence, wanting to stay in the discipline, or feeling valued
- Peer observation rubrics and quotes
- Survey data related to student perceptions
- Audiovisual clips of exemplary teaching moments

We began this chapter with a fictitious scenario in which your teaching statement read "I create an inclusive classroom environment," with no other words referring to how this conclusion was reached. We hope that at this point in the book, you have had time to develop and refine your own ideas about what this statement means, how you put it into practice, and how you show others it is true.

Opportunities for Inclusion in Every Moment

Exclusion is often easy to identify and define.

> A student raises her hand to volunteer an answer to the professor's question to the whole class: "The end of the Civil War."
>
> Professor #1 responds: "No, not at all correct. Did you even do the homework?"

In this example, this student has been shamed and the other students in the classroom will hesitate to contribute, for fear that they too will be shamed. However, the absence of exclusion is not necessarily inclusion. Inclusion requires intentional effort. Inclusion may be more difficult to identify and name. Let's revisit the scenario with a professor being more intentional.

> A student raises her hand to volunteer an answer to the professor's question to the whole class: "The end of the Civil War."
>
> Professor #2 responds: "Thank you, Maya. This is a common perception and a great opportunity to learn. Let's all take a moment in our groups to discuss why many of you likely came to this same conclusion and what we need to know to collectively improve the answer."

These are not words spoken by simply a nice professor, a word students may use to describe this professor. This professor is more than nice. They intentionally use this language with the hope this student sees that she is not alone and that there is value to her contribution. She and others get the message that mistakes are a normal and useful part of learning. Thus, the second professor's response is grounded in scholarly ideas of student belonging and growth mind-set. This moment in a classroom, which plays out in just a few seconds, is an example of the millions of moments happening in higher education at all times.

Our own journey through teaching has taught us to be like Professor #2. While we were never like Professor #1, we weren't always thinking about every moment as an opportunity to go beyond being neutral. We have a different mind-set now, one that we've cultivated through many years of practice and reflection to be intentional about inclusion in every way a student interacts with our course and us.

We feel empowered knowing that our course designs, words, and actions have helped a myriad of students find our disciplines to be "not as bad as they thought," do well in our courses, get their first research opportunities, find a friend in our classroom, be the first to graduate from college in their families, thrive during a difficult period in young adulthood, find a mentor, enter a medical or graduate school program, and so much more. We want to be your reminder that, as an educator, what you do is valuable to each and every student. Ultimately, your teaching is much more far-reaching as it impacts how students navigate the world beyond our classroom. We can serve as a model of what inclusion looks and feels like.

We believe that diversity, equity, and inclusion work won't be successful until it is the work of everyone in the community and not just a dedicated committee. It is the responsibility of *all* of us as educators to help students embrace diversity, identify inequities in the world around them, and remove barriers when they can. As educators, every interaction we have has the potential to be meaningful and impactful. We hope that we've empowered you to see the influence you hold in helping to shape a more just world—one student at a time.

INSTRUCTOR CHECKLIST

Self-reflection:

- Make quick daily reflections though notes and voice memos.
- Record your teaching and watch it. Audio files can be useful for sound analysis.
- Consider making a customized daily/weekly self-reflection form to encourage good habits.

Student feedback:

- Collect informal micro-feedback through polls, thumbs up/thumbs down, questions within assignments, and continuously available anonymous surveys.
- Design a midsemester survey to collect more formal feedback.
- Add questions to an end-of-course evaluation if possible.
- Conduct focus groups with students, facilitated by you or a colleague.
- Curate unsolicited feedback.
- Teach students how to give useful feedback and explain why it's valuable to you.
- Use the last day of class to allow students to reflect on their growth, reinforce the growth mind-set, invite students to be lifelong learners in your discipline, bridge their academic skills with professional skills, and write notes of advice to future students.

Peer feedback:

- Identify colleagues who can provide formative feedback for learning, as opposed to summative high-stakes feedback related to employment and career track.
- Provide your peer reviewers access to course materials in addition to inviting them to your class.
- Ask to meet with peers briefly before and after the review.
- Provide a rubric or ask for specific kinds of feedback related to inclusive strategies such as your use of non-content instructor talk.

Informative data:

- Collect data from students about their perceptions, behaviors, and knowledge-related diversity and inclusion; consider a pre- and post- survey or student samples of work at the beginning and end of term to measure change.
- Request demographic data for students you have taught; reflect on the diversity of your students as well as disparities in performance for certain student groups.

Curating evidence for a dossier:

- Don't wait until you need to put a dossier together to collect evidence of your commitment to inclusive teaching.
- Curate student quotes, self-reflections, examples of assignments, exemplary student work, recordings, syllabi, surveys, and peer observations.

ACKNOWLEDGMENTS

We want to thank Jim Lang for recognizing the work we were doing and inviting us to share it with a wider audience of readers. Jim, thank you for your continual encouragement and feedback on drafts. Jim also welcomed us into the WVU Teaching and Learning in Higher Education Series author team—what a wonderful group of people, who are a wealth of knowledge and passion. Thanks also to Derek Krissoff and others at WVU Press.

Bob Henshaw at UNC's Center for Faculty Excellence has been a valuable colleague and friend to both of us since we began teaching. We thank him for all he has done to help us develop as teachers and professionals and for reading a draft of the book. Our mentor and friend, Abigail, has always modeled systems-level thinking about student success, and we thank for her for all she has taught us. Thank you also to Carly Schnitzler, Eric Hastie, and Erica Bossen for some helpful reviewing during final stages of writing.

We would like to acknowledge some of the people who have inspired a lot of our work together. We find ourselves drawn to and in agreement with anything Kimberly Tanner at San Francisco State University and her colleagues produce. Similarly, Scott Freeman and Sarah Eddy have provided mentorship and collaborations in the past that have immensely influenced our thoughts about structure in the classroom.

Collaborating through a pandemic limited some of the physical time we could be together and meant many of our joint sessions were on one of our porches. LaCroix provided the refreshment and got us through some very warm North Carolina summer days and one or two beach writing retreats.

There are countless faculty at various institutions who helped us hone our thinking and tighten our messages as we gave workshops and listened to their questions. We thank all the institutions that have invited us and given us the chance to present our ideas and learn from these interactions.

We want to thank the people who champion our work. On our own campus: Deborah Clarke, Buck Goldstein, Kevin Guskiewicz, and Todd Zakrajzek. We are grateful to our Center for Faculty Excellence for bringing us together and supporting our development. We've also benefited from the support of past leadership at UNC: Carol Folt and Holden Thorp. We are grateful to Emily Miller at the Association of American Universities. We have benefited from conversations we've had with colleagues who have brought us in for HHMI Inclusive Excellence grants and institutions that have partnered with ACUE. We have had the great pleasure to interact with many champions on Twitter—too many to name.

Not all of our efforts have been smoothly paved, but even these have only made us more resolute in our work. With fortitude and a robust support system, we researched and wrote a book in many in-between moments over several years. There were no sabbaticals or other infrastructures to support a couple of non-tenured teaching faculty, women in STEM, and mothers, in producing scholarship such as this. We are proud of what we have produced despite these obstacles. We don't want this book to be proof that it can be done, instead we want it to be an example of what might see the light of day if there were more supportive structures in place for a diverse group of educators who have the drive to share their expertise.

Combined, we have taught so many students over the years they could populate a small city. Our students pushed us to do better and learn about diversity and inclusion, not because they demanded it but because their excellence deserved it. Through every interaction we had with students in groups and one-on-one, we learned valuable lessons about inclusion. Thank you, Carolina students.

Kelly has a few notes of thanks, beginning with Viji. She and Viji have been two peas in a pod since the day they met. They formed an invaluable professional and personal friendship based on the best similarities and differences! Kelly also acknowledges the many people in her department leadership that gave her space to be both creative and a leader in her teaching, and she recognizes the numerous colleagues, especially Jean DeSaix, and students she has learned from along the way. Kelly thanks her mother, Vivian, and sister, Tracey, for their continual daily support and encouragement in her ability to take on new challenges. Preparing to be a teacher started at an early age for Kelly when she played school with her sister, perhaps because she was jealous that her older sister never let her play the role of teacher! Other teacher role models to recognize in her life include Aunt Marie and her father, plus the numerous teachers from kindergarten through PhD utilizing strategies she has inevitably taken into her own teaching. Kelly loves her two children, Jake and Lexi, who have put up with a mother who has a laptop on her lap too often and do their best to prioritize their mother's wishes for a family dinner at the end of each busy day. Lastly, immense gratitude and love goes from Kelly to her husband for his unending belief that his wife can do anything.

Viji would like to thank her co-author, colleague, and dear friend Kelly Hogan. What a tremendous ride we've been on, and I look forward to paving new paths with you—fizzy water at hand. Viji thanks her parents and brother, Ram, Meena, and Kumar Sathy. From an early age her parents instilled in Viji and Kumar the transformative power of a good education and they did everything they could including moving half-way around the world for better opportunities for their children. Viji would also like to thank her bonus family for never-ending encouragement: Connie and Elliot Bossen, Charlotte and Henry Moore. Viji has benefited from many wonderful public educators in NC from Kindergraten through a PhD. In particular, she would like to thank her first statistics professor and now dear friend, Abigail Panter ("Dr. P"). Dr. P modeled what it meant to be an inclusive educator. Much of what Viji incorporated in her own teaching was to emulate the thought and care that Abigail showed her students and colleagues. Viji would like to thank her partner, Quinn Moore, who didn't just say "you can do it," but he did all the things that needed to be done at home so that she could do this and more. Lastly, Viji thanks her kids, Ori and Valen. They were tiny when her teaching career began and now they are not! They never once begrudged her for her work and literally grew up hearing her talk about equity in education. She hopes that in seeing this book to fruition and potentially impacting more students than her own, they see that one person can push for a more just world – at least in their corner of the world.

Finally, we both thank you, our readers. You picked up a book about teaching. We hope you will take ideas that work for you. More importantly, we hope that you add to these ideas or conduct scholarship that helps us all become more inclusive educators. We are grateful you are dedicating some time to the craft of teaching and thank you for supporting students in your corner of the world. It seems that a couple of quiet women in STEM can have a few things to say and that there are more than a few who will listen. Thank you for joining us in what we hope will be an ongoing conversation about equity.

REFERENCES

Aguillon, Stepfanie M., Gregor-Fausto Siegmund, Renee H. Petipas, Abby Grace Drake, Sehoya Cotner, & Cissy J. Ballen. (2020). Gender differences in student participation in an active-learning classroom. *CBE—Life Sciences Education*, 19(2), Article 12. https://doi.org /10.1187/cbe.19-03-0048

Akechi, Hironori, Atsushi Senju, Helen Uibo, Yukiko Kikuchi, Toshikazu Hasegawa, & Jari K. Hietanen. (2013). Attention to eye contact in the west and east: Autonomic responses and evaluative ratings. *PLOS ONE*, 8(3). https://doi.org/10.1371/journal.pone.0059312

Allen, Deborah, & Kimberly Tanner. (2006). Rubrics: Tools for making learning goals and evaluation criteria explicit for both teachers and learners. *CBE—Life Sciences Education*. https://doi.org/10.1187 /cbe.06-06-0168

Ambady, Nalini, & Robert Rosenthal. (1993). Half a minute: Predicting teacher evaluations from thin slices of nonverbal behavior and physical attractiveness. *Journal of Personality and Social Psychology*, 64(3), 431–41. https://doi.org/10.1037/0022-3514.64.3.431

American Association for the Advancement of Science. (2011). Vision and change in undergraduate biology education: A call to action. https:// live-visionandchange.pantheonsite.io/wp-content/uploads/2011/03 /Revised-Vision-and-Change-Final-Report.pdf

American Council on Education. (2019). Race and ethnicity in higher education. https://www.equityinhighered.org/indicators/enrollment-in -undergraduate-education/

Ariely, Dan, & Klaus Wertenbroch. (2002). Procrastination, deadlines, and performance: Self-control by precommitment. *Psychological Science*, 13(3), 219–24. https://doi.org/10.1111/1467-9280.00441

Association of American Colleges and Universities. (n.d.). VALUE. https:// www.aacu.org/value

Auchincloss, Lisa Corwin, Sandra L. Laursen, Janet L. Branchaw, Kevin Eagan, Mark Graham, David I. Hanauer, Gwendolyn Lawrie, et al. (2014). Assessment of course-based undergraduate research experiences: A meeting report. *CBE—Life Sciences Education*, 13(1), 29–40. https://doi.org/10.1187/cbe.14-01-0004

Babad, Elisha, Dinah Avni-Babad, & Robert Rosenthal. (2004). Prediction of students' evaluations from brief instances of professors' nonverbal behavior in defined instructional situations. *Social Psychology of Education,* 7(1), 3–33. https://doi.org/10.1023/B:SPOE .0000010672.97522.c5

Bangera, Gita, & Sara E. Brownell. (2014). Course-based undergraduate research experiences can make scientific research more inclusive. *CBE—Life Sciences Education,* 13(4), 602–6. https://doi.org/10.1187 /cbe.14-06-0099

Barre, Betsy, Allen Brown, & Justin Esarey. (n.d.). Course workload estimator, 2.0. https://cat.wfu.edu/resources/tools/estimator2/

Berk, Ronald A. (2000). "Does humor in course tests reduce anxiety and improve performance? *College Teaching,* 48(4), 151–58. https://doi .org/10.1080/87567550009595834

Bowers, Sacharitha. [@SBowersMD]. (2019, November 3*). #Microaggression tip* [Tweet]. Twitter. https://twitter.com/sbowersmd/status /1191029251182661638?s=11

Brame, Cynthia J. (2013). Writing good multiple choice test questions. https://cft.vanderbilt.edu/guides-sub-pages/writing-good-multiple -choice-test-questions/

British Dyslexia Association. (n.d.). Dyslexia friendly style guide. https:// www.bdadyslexia.org.uk/advice/employers/creating-a-dyslexia-friendly -workplace/dyslexia-friendly-style-guide

Brown, Peter C., Henry L. Roediger III, & Mark A. McDaniel. (2014). *Make it stick: The science of successful learning.* Belknap Press of Harvard University Press.

Brown University, Harriet W. Sheridan Center for Teaching and Learning. (n.d.). Diversity & inclusion syllabus statements. https://www.brown .edu/sheridan/teaching-learning-resources/inclusive-teaching /statements

Bruff, Derek. (2009). *Teaching with classroom response systems: Creating active learning environments.* Jossey-Bass.

———. (2015, September 15). In defense of continuous exposition by the teacher. *Agile Learning.* https://derekbruff.org/?p=3126

———. (2019). *Intentional Tech: Principles to Guide the Use of Educational Technology in College Teaching.* West Virginia University Press.

Canning, Elizabeth A., Katherine Muenks, Dorainne J. Green, & Mary C. Murphy. (2019). STEM faculty who believe ability is fixed have larger racial achievement gaps and inspire less student motivation in their classes. *Science Advances,* 5(2). https://doi.org/10.1126/sciadv.aau4734

Casper, Anne M., Sarah L. Eddy, & Scott Freeman. (2019). True grit: Passion and persistence make an innovative course design work. *PLOS Biology,* 17(7), Article e3000359. https://doi.org/10.1371/journal.pbio .3000359

CAST. (2018). Universal design for learning guidelines version 2.2. https:// www.cast.org/impact/universal-design-for-learning-udl

Cavanagh, Sarah Rose. (2016). *The spark of learning: Energizing the college classroom with the science of emotion.* West Virginia University Press.

—. (2019, May 5). The best (and worst) ways to respond to student anxiety. *The Chronicle of Higher Education*. https://www.chronicle.com/article/The-Best-and-Worst-Ways-to/246226

Cayanus, Jacob L. (2004). Effective instructional practice: Using teacher self-disclosure as an instructional tool. *Communication Teacher,* 18(1), 6–9. https://doi.org/10.1080/1740462032000142095

Chi, Michelene T. H., & Ruth Wylie. (2014). The ICAP framework: Linking cognitive engagement to active learning outcomes. *Educational Psychologist,* 49(4), 219–43. https://doi.org/10.1080/00461520.2014.965823

Cooper, Katelyn M., & Sara E. Brownell. (2016). Coming out in class: Challenges and benefits of active learning in a biology classroom for LGBTQIA students. *CBE—Life Sciences Education,*15(3), Article 37. https://doi.org/10.1187/cbe.16-01-0074

Cooper, Katelyn M., Brian Haney, Anna Krieg, & Sara E. Brownell. (2017a). What's in a name? The importance of students perceiving that an instructor knows their names in a high-enrollment biology classroom. *CBE—Life Sciences Education,*16 (1), Article 8. https://doi.org/10.1187/cbe.16-08-0265

Cooper, Katelyn M., Jeffrey N. Schinske, & Kimberly D. Tanner. (2021). Reconsidering the share of a think–pair–share: Emerging limitations, alternatives, and opportunities for research. *CBE— Life Sciences Education,* 20(1), 1–10. https://doi.org/10.1187/cbe.20-08-0200

Costa, Karen. (2020, May 27). *Cameras be damned.* [Post] Linkedin. https://www.linkedin.com/pulse/cameras-damned-karen-costa

Cullen, Roxanne, & Michael Harris. (2009). Assessing learner-centredness through course syllabi. *Assessment & Evaluation in Higher Education,* 34(1), 115–25. https://doi.org/10.1080/02602930801956018

Dallimore, Elise J., Julie H. Hertenstein, & Marjorie B. Platt. (2013). Impact of cold-calling on student voluntary participation. *Journal of Management Education,* 37(3), 305–41. https://doi.org/10.1177/1052562912446067

Darby, Flower, & James M. Lang. (2019). *Small teaching online: Applying learning science in online classes.* Jossey-Bass.

Dechavez, Yvette. (2018, October 8). It's time to decolonize that syllabus. *Los Angeles Times*. https://www.latimes.com/books/la-et-jc-decolonize-syllabus-20181008-story.html

Deslauriers, Louis, Ellen Schelew, & Carl Wieman. (2011). Improved learning in a large-enrollment physics class. *Science*, 332(6031), 862–64. https://doi.org/10.1126/science.1201783

Dewsbury, Bryan, & Cynthia J. Brame. (2019). Inclusive teaching. *CBE—Life Sciences Education* 18(2). https://doi.org/10.1187/cbe.19-01-0021

DiBattista, David, Jo Anne Sinnige-Egger, & Glenda Fortuna. (2014). The "none of the above" option in multiple-choice testing: An experimental study. *Journal of Experimental Education,* 82(2), 168–83. https://doi.org/10.1080/00220973.2013.79512

Dukes, Richard L., & Heather Albanesi. (2013). Seeing red: Quality of an essay, color of the grading pen, and student reactions to the grading process. *Social Science Journal, 50*(1), 96–100. https://doi.org/10.1016 /j.soscij.2012.07.005

Dunlea, Michael. (2019, September 4). Every student matters: Cultivating belonging in the classroom. *Edutopia.* https://www.edutopia.org /article/every-student-matters-cultivating-belonging-classroom

Dweck, Carol. (1999). *Self-Theories: Their Role in Motivation, Personality, and Development.* Routledge.

———. (2006). *Mindset: The New Psychology of Success.* Random House.

Eagan, M. Kevin, Sylvia Hurtado, Mitchell J. Chang, Gina A. Garcia, Felisha A. Herrera, & Juan C. Garibay. (2013). Making a difference in science education. *American Educational Research Journal, 50*(4), 683–713. http://journals.sagepub.com/doi/10.3102/0002831213482038

Eddy, Sarah L., Sara E. Brownell, Phonraphee Thummaphan, Ming-Chih Lan, & Mary Pat Wenderoth. (2015). Caution, student experience may vary: Social identities impact a student's experience in peer discussions. *CBE—Life Sciences Education, 14*(4), Article 45. https:// doi.org/10.1187/cbe.15-05-0108

Eddy, Sarah L., Sara E. Brownell, & Mary Pat Wenderoth. (2014). Gender gaps in achievement and participation in multiple introductory biology classrooms. *CBE—Life Sciences Education, 13*(3), 478–92. https://doi .org/10.1187/cbe.13-10-0204

Eddy, Sarah L., & Kelly A. Hogan. (2014). Getting under the hood: How and for whom does increasing course structure work? *CBE—Life Sciences Education, 13*(3), 453–68. https://doi.org/10.1187/cbe.14-03-0050

Eyler, Joshua R. (2018). *How humans learn: The science and stories behind effective college teaching.* West Virginia University Press.

Feldberg-Dubin, Hannah. (2016, June). *Top 11 skills of an effective facilitator.* The Design Gym. https://www.thedesigngym.com/top-11-skills -effective-facilitator/

Felder, Richard M., & Rebecca Brent. (2016). *Teaching and learning STEM: A practical guide.* Jossey-Bass.

Felton, Peter. (2019, October 21). Creating a "relentless welcome." *Teaching Matters.* https://www.teaching-matters-blog.ed.ac.uk/creating-a -relentless-welcome/

Fiock, Holly, & Heather Garcia. (2019, November 15). How to give your students better feedback with technology. *The Chronicle of Higher Education.* https://www.chronicle.com/interactives/20191108 -Advice-Feedback

Fleurizard, Tyrone. (2018, July 20). How to deal with microaggressions in class [Opinion]. *Inside Higher Ed.* https://www.insidehighered.com /advice/2018/07/20/how-deal-microaggressions-class-opinion

Freeman, Scott, Sarah L. Eddy, Miles McDonough, Michelle K. Smith, Nnadozie Okoroafor, Hannah Jordt, & Mary Pat Wenderoth. (2014). Active learning increases student performance in science, engineering, and mathematics. *Proceedings of the National Academy of Sciences of the United States of America,* 111(23), 8410–15. https://doi.org/10.1073/pnas.1319030111

Freeman, Scott, David Haak, & Mary Pat Wenderoth. (2011). Increased course structure improves performance in introductory biology. *CBE—Life Sciences Education* 10(2), 175–86. https://doi.org/10.1187/cbe.10-08-0105

Gannon, Kevin. (2019, August 16). How to create a syllabus. *The Chronicle of Higher Education.* https://www.chronicle.com/interactives/advice-syllabus

———. (2019, September). The syllabus from a student perspective. *The Tattooed Professor.* http://www.thetattooedprof.com/wp-content/uploads/2019/09/The-Syllabus-from-a-student-perspective.pdf

———. (2020). *Radical hope: A teaching manifesto.* West Virginia University Press.

Gin, Logan E., Ashley A. Rowland, Blaire Steinwand, John Bruno, & Lisa A. Corwin. (2018). Students who fail to achieve predefined research goals may still experience many positive outcomes as a result of CURE participation. *CBE—Life Sciences Education,* 17(4), Article 57. https://doi.org/10.1187/cbe.18-03-0036

Goldrick-Rab, Sara. (2017, August 7). *Basic needs security and the syllabus.* Medium. https://medium.com/@saragoldrickrab/basic-needs-security-and-the-syllabus-d24cc7afe8c9

Griffin, Whitney, Steven D. Cohen, Rachel Berndtson, Kristen M. Burson, K. Martin Camper, Yujie Chen, & Margaret Austin Smith. (2014). Starting the conversation: An exploratory study of factors that influence student office hour use. *College Teaching,* 62(3), 94–99. https://doi.org/10.1080/87567555.2014.896777

Grunspan, Daniel Z., Sarah L. Eddy, Sara E. Brownell, Benjamin L. Wiggins, Alison J. Crowe, & Steven M. Goodreau. (2016). Males under-estimate academic performance of their female peers in undergraduate biology classrooms. *PLOS ONE,* 11(2), e0148405. https://doi.org/10.1371/journal.pone.0148405

Hahn, Sabrina. (2019, September 9). Part I: Achievement gap, or opportunity gap? What's stopping student success [Radio broadcast]. WBUR, On Point. https://www.wbur.org/onpoint/2019/09/09/achievement-gap-opportunity-education-schools-students-teachers

Haladyna, Thomas M., & Steven M. Downing. (1989). A taxonomy of multiple choice item-writing rules. *Applied Measurement in Education,* 2(1), 37–50. https://doi.org/10.1207/s15324818ame0201_3

Haladyna, Thomas M., Steven M. Downing, & Michael C. Rodriguez. (2002). A review of multiple-choice item-writing guidelines for classroom assessment. *Applied Measurement in Education.* Lawrence Erlbaum Associates. https://doi.org/10.1207/s15324818ame1503_5

Harnish, Richard J., & K. Robert Bridges. (2011). Effect of syllabus tone: Students' perceptions of instructor and course. *Social Psychology of*

Education, 14(3), 319–30. https://doi.org/10.1007/s11218-011 –9152-4

Hogan, Kelly, & Viji Sathy. (2019, March 27). How an inclusive teaching approach helped us build a more inclusive curriculum for our university. *ACUE.* https://community.acue.org/blog/inclusive-curriculum/

Howard, Jay R. (2019). How to hold a better class discussion. *The Chronicle of Higher Education.* https://www.chronicle.com/interactives /20190523-ClassDiscussion

Howard, Jay R., & Roberta Baird. (2000). The consolidation of responsibility and students' definitions of situation in the mixed-age college classroom. *The Journal of Higher Education,* 71, 700–72.

Huber, Mary Taylor, Pat Hutchings, Richard Gale, Ross Miller, & Molly Breen. (2007, Spring). Leading initiatives for integrative learning. *Liberal Education*, 93(2), 46–51. www.carnegiefoundation.org/e -library/

Hughes, Bryce E, Sylvia Hurtado, & M. Kevin Eagan. (2014, November). Driving up or dialing down competition in introductory STEM courses: Individual and classroom level factors. Association for the Study of Higher Education. https://www.heri.ucla.edu/nih/downloads /ASHE2014-Competition-in-Introductory-STEM-Courses.pdf

Hurtado, Sylvia, Kevin M. Eagan & Mitchell J. Chang. (2010, January). Degrees of success: Bachelor's degree completion rates among initial STEM majors. Higher Education Research Institute at UCLA.

Imad, Mays. (2020, June 3). Leveraging the neuroscience of now. *Inside Higher Ed*. https://www.insidehighered.com/advice/2020/06/03 /seven-recommendations-helping-students-thrive-times-trauma

Inclusive Excellence. (n.d.) https://www.hhmi.org/science-education /programs/inclusive-excellence-new-competition-announcement

Kansas State Department of Education. (n.d.). Module 4: Activity 2: Avoiding test bias. Assessment Literacy Project.

Karp, David A., & William C. Yoels. (1976). The college classroom: Some observations on the meaning of student participation. *Sociology and Social Research,* 60, 421–39.

Karpicke, Jeffrey D., & Henry L. Roediger. (2007). Expanding retrieval practice promotes short-term retention, but equally spaced retrieval enhances long-term retention. *Journal of Experimental Psychology: Learning, Memory, and Cognition,* 33(4), 704–19. https://doi.org /10.1037/0278-7393.33.4.704

Kernahan, Cyndi. (2019). *Teaching about race and racism in the college classroom*. West Virginia University Press.

Kharbach, Med. (2018, January 16). *5 of the best rubric making tools for teachers*. Educational Technology and Mobile Learning. https://www .educatorstechnology.com/2018/01/5-of-best-rubric-making-tools-for .html

Kimball, Miles, Noah Smith, & Quartz. (2013, October 28). The myth of "I'm bad at math." *The Atlantic*. https://www.theatlantic.com/education/archive/2013/10/the-myth-of-im-bad-at-math/280914/

Knight, Jennifer K., Sarah B. Wise, & Katelyn M. Southard. (2013). Understanding clicker discussions: Student reasoning and the impact of instructional cues. *CBE—Life Sciences Education, 12*(4), 645–54. https://doi.org/10.1187/cbe.13-05-0090

Kohli, Rita, & Daniel G. Solórzano. (2012). Teachers, please learn our names! Racial microaggressions and the K-12 classroom. *Race and Ethnicity Education,* 14(4), 441–62.

Korzik, Morgan L., Hannah M. Austin, Brittany Cooper, Caroline Jaspersde, Grace Tan, Emilie Richards, Erin T. Spencer, Blaire Steinwand, F. Joel Fodrie, & John F. Bruno. (2019, August 31). Marketplace shrimp mislabeling in North Carolina. PLoS ONE 15(3): e0229512. https://doi.org/10.1371/journal.pone.0229512

Kreitzer, Rebecca J., & Jennie Sweet-Cushman. (2021, February 9). Evaluating student evaluations of teaching: A review of measurement and equity bias in SETs and recommendations for ethical reform. *Journal of Academic Ethics,* 1–12. https://doi.org/10.1007/S10805-021-09400-W

Kuh, George D., & Shouping Hu. (2001, Spring). The effects of student-faculty interaction in the 1990s. *Review of Higher Education,* 24(3), 309–32. https://doi.org/10.1353/rhe.2001.0005

Kwong, Emily, Madeline K. Sofia, & Rebecca Ramirez (Hosts). (2020, October 1). Want to dismantle racism in science? Start in the classroom. [Audio podcast episode]. In National Public Radio *Short Wave.* https://www.npr.org/2020/09/30/918864226/want-to-dismantle-racism-in-science-start-in-the-classroom

Landhuis, Esther. (2019, June 1). Making STEM education more welcoming to underrepresented minorities. *The Scientist.* https://www.the-scientist.com/careers/making-stem-education-more-welcoming-to-underrepresented-minorities-65910

Lang, James M. (2016a, May 16). Small changes in teaching: Space it out. *The Chronicle of Higher Education.* https://www.chronicle.com/package/small-changes-in-teaching/

———. (2016b). *Small teaching: Everyday lessons from the science of learning.* Jossey-Bass.

———. (2020). *Distracted: Why students can't focus and what you can do about it.* Basic Books.

———. (2020, November 16). Distracted minds: The role of tempo in good teaching. *The Chronicle of Higher Education.* https://www.chronicle.com/article/distracted-minds-the-role-of-tempo-in-good-teaching

Lepper, Mark, & Maria Woolverton. (2002). The wisdom of practice: Lessons learned from the study of highly effective tutors. In J. Aronson (Ed.), Improving academic achievement: Impact of psychological factors on education (pp. 135–58). Academic Press. https://doi.org/10.1016 /B978-012064455-1/50010-5

Limbong, Andrew. (2020, June 9). *What is a microaggression? And what to do if you experience one* [Radio broadcast]. NPR Life Kit. https://www.npr .org/2020/06/08/872371063/microaggressions-are-a-big-deal-how-to -talk-them-out-and-when-to-walk-away

Malouff, John M., Ashley J. Emmerton, & Nicola S. Schutte. (2013, May 8). The risk of a halo bias as a reason to keep students anonymous during grading. *Teaching of Psychology.* https://doi.org/10.1177 /0098628313487425

Malouff, John M, & Einar B. Thorsteinsson. (2016). Bias in grading: A meta-analysis of experimental research findings. *Australian Journal of Education,* 60(3), 245–56. https://doi.org/10.1177/0004944116664618

May, Cindi. (2017, July 11). Students are better off without a laptop in the classroom. *Scientific American.* https://www.scientificamerican.com /article/students-are-better-off-without-a-laptop-in-the-classroom/

McKenna, Laura. (2018, February). How hard do professors actually work? *The Atlantic.* https://www.theatlantic.com/education/archive/2018/02 /how-hard-do-professors-actually-work/552698/

Meij, Hans van der, & Linn Böckmann. (2021). Effects of embedded questions in recorded lectures. *Journal of Computing in Higher Education,* 33(1), 235–54. https://doi.org/10.1007/s12528 -020-09263-x

Merculieff, Ilarion, & Libby Roderick. (2013). *Stop talking. Indigenous ways of teaching and learning and difficult dialogues in higher education.* University of Alaska Anchorage. https://www.uaa.alaska.edu /academics/office-of-academic-affairs/faculty-development -instructional-support/center-for-advancing-faculty-excellence /difficult-dialogues/_documents/Stop_Talking.pdf

Merriam-Webster. (2021). Exclude. In *Merriam-Webster.com dictionary.* https://www.merriam-webster.com/dictionary/exclude

Miller, Meg. (2017, March 8). This app uses AI to track mansplaining in your meetings. *Fast Company,* 2017. https://www.fastcompany.com /3068794/this-app-uses-ai-to-track-mansplaining-during -your-meetings

Miller, Michelle. (2014). *Minds online: Teaching effectively with technology.* Harvard University Press.

Mollin, Sam. (2018, March 29). Grading on a curve promotes toxic competition. *The John Hopkins News-Letter.*

Mt. Holyoke College, Center for Teaching and Learning. (n.d.). Sample civility statements. https://www.mtholyoke.edu/sites/default/files /teachinglearninginitiatives/docs/civilitysamples.pdf

Mulliner, Emma, & Matthew Tucker. (2017). Feedback on feedback practice: Perceptions of students and academics. *Assessment and Evaluation in Higher Education,* 42(2), 266–88. https://doi.org/10.1080 /02602938.2015.1103365

Murthy, Vivek. (2020). *Together: The healing power of human connection in a sometimes lonely world*. Harper Wave.

Nadworny, Elissa. (2018, December 12). *"Going to office hours is terrifying" and other tales of rural students in college* [Radio broadcast]. NPR Morning Edition. https://www.npr.org/2018/12/12/668530699 /-going-to-office-hours-is-terrifying-and-other-hurdles-for-rural -students-in-col

————. (2019, October 6). *College students: How to make office hours less scary* [Radio broadcast]. WAMU/ NPR. https://wamu.org/story/19 /10/06/college-students-how-to-make-office-hours-less-scary/.

National Academies of Sciences, Engineering, and Medicine. (2016). *Barriers and opportunities for 2-year and 4-year STEM degrees: Systemic change to support students' diverse pathways*. National Academies Press. https://doi.org/10.17226/21739

Neuhaus, Jessamyn. (2019). *Geeky Pedagogy: A Guide for Intellectuals, Introverts, and Nerds Who Want to Be Effective Teachers*. West Virginia University Press.

Nilson, Linda. (2015). *Specifications grading: Restoring rigor, motivating students, and saving faculty time*. Stylus Publishing.

NYU School of Law. (n.d.). Grading system and academic standards. https://www.law.nyu.edu/academicservices/academic-policies /grading-system-academic-standards

Oakes, Lisa. @oakeslisa. (2019, February 6). *Interesting. I have a small laptop zone in my class* [Tweet]. Twitter. https://twitter.com/oakeslisa /status/1093185400410009600

Ohlin, Birgit. (2020, April 12). *Active listening: Why empathetic conversation matters*. PositivePsychology.com. https://positivepsychology.com /active-listening/

Owen, Ann. (2019, June 24). The next lawsuits to hit higher education [Opinion]. *Inside Higher Ed*. https://www.insidehighered.com/views /2019/06/24/relying-often-biased-student-evaluations-assess-faculty -could-lead-lawsuits-opinion

Owens, Melinda T., Shannon B. Seidel, Mike Wong, Travis E. Bejines, Susanne Lietz, Joseph R. Perez, Shangheng Sit, et al. (2017). Classroom sound can be used to classify teaching practices in college science courses. *Proceedings of the National Academy of Sciences of the United States of America*, 114(12), 3085–90. https://doi.org/10.1073/pnas .1618693114

Palmer, Robert T., Dina C. Maramba, & T. Elon Dancy II. (2011, Fall). A qualitative investigation of factors promoting the retention and persistence of students of color in STEM. *Journal of Negro Education*, 80(4), 491–504. https://www.jstor.org/stable/41341155

Parker, Priya. (2020). *The art of gathering: How we meet and why it matters*. Riverhead Books.

Patterson, Bailey. (2019). Welcome to Carol Folt's $4.25B Memorial Meme Stash (UNC) [Facebook page]. Facebook.

Penn State University Faculty Senate. (2021, July 16 [revised]). Syllabus statement examples. https://senate.psu.edu/faculty/syllabus -statement-examples/

Penner, Marsha R., Viji Sathy, & Kelly A. Hogan. (2021,April 17). Inclusion in neuroscience through high impact courses. *Neuroscience Letters* 750, Article 135740. https://doi.org/10.1016/J.NEULET.2021.135740

Petersen, Christina I., Paul Baepler, Al Beitz, Paul Ching, Kristen S. Gorman, Cheryl L. Neudauer, William Rozaitis, J. D. Walker, & Deb Wingert. (2020). The tyranny of content: "Content coverage" as a barrier to evidence-based teaching approaches and ways to overcome it. *CBE—Life Sciences Education,* 19(2), Article 17. https://doi.org /10.1187/cbe.19-04-0079

Phillips, Katherine W. (2014, October 4). How diversity works. *Scientific American,* 311(4), 42–47. https://doi.org/10.1038/scientific american1014-42

Pryal, Katie Rose Guest, & Jordynn Jack. (2017, November 27). *When you talk about banning laptops, you throw disabled students under the bus.* HuffPost. https://www.huffpost.com/entry/when-you-talk-about -banning-laptops-you-throw-disabled_b_5a1ccb4ee4b07bcab2c6997d

Patel, Raisa. (2019, January 3). *Here's how to pronounce my name, and why it matters to me* [Radio broadcast]. *CBC News-Radio Canada.*

Ramey, Jessie B. (2019, March 20). A note from your colleagues with hearing loss: Just use a microphone already. *The Chronicle of Higher Education.* https://www.chronicle.com/article/A-Note-From-Your -Colleagues/245916

Reynolds, Garr. (2012). *Presentation Zen design: A simple visual approach to presenting in today's world* (2nd ed.). New Riders.

Richmond, Aaron S., Jeanne M. Slattery, Nathanael Mitchell, Robin K. Morgan, & Jared Becknell. (2016). Can a learner-centered syllabus change students' perceptions of student–professor rapport and master teacher behaviors? *Scholarship of Teaching and Learning in Psychology,* 2(3), 159–68. https://doi.org/10.1037/stl0000066

Roberson, Robin. (2013, September). *Helping students find relevance.* American Psychological Association. https://www.apa.org/ed /precollege/ptn/2013/09/students-relevance

Rock, David, & Heidi Grant. (2016, November 4). Why diverse teams are smarter. *Harvard Business Review.* https://hbr.org/2016/11/why -diverse-teams-are-smarter

Rodriguez, Michael C., & Anthony D. Albano. (2017). *The college instructor's guide to writing test items: Measuring student learning.* Routledge.

Roth, Don. (2007). Understanding by design: A framework for effecting curricular development and assessment. *CBE—Life Sciences Education,* 6(2), 95–97. https://doi.org/10.1187/cbe.07-03-0012

Sana, Faria, Tina Weston, & Nicholas J. Cepeda. (2013, March). Laptop multitasking hinders classroom learning for both users and nearby peers. *Computers and Education* 62, 24–31. https://doi.org/10.1016 /j.compedu.2012.10.003

Sathy, Viji, & Kelly A. Hogan. (2020). *Sample syllabi statements.* InclusifiED. https://sites.google.com/view/inclusified/sample-syllabus-statements

Sathy, Viji, & Quinn Moore. (2020, July 14). Who benefits from the flipped classroom? Quasi-experimental findings on student learning, engagement, course perceptions and interest in statistics. In J. Rodgers Taylor-Francis, ed, *Teaching Statistics and Qualitative Methods in the 21st Century*, Multivariate Analysis Series.

Sathy, Viji, Chris L. Strauss, Mahfuz Nasiri, A. T. Panter, Kelly A. Hogan, & Bryant L. Hutson. (2020, August). Cultivating inclusive research experiences through course-based curriculum. *Scholarship of Teaching and Learning in Psychology*. https://doi.org/10.1037/STL0000215

Schinske, Jeffrey N., Heather Perkins, Amanda Snyder, & Mary Wyer. (2016). Scientist spotlight homework assignments shift students' stereotypes of scientists and enhance science identity in a diverse introductory science class. *CBE—Life Sciences Education,* 15(3), Article 47. https://doi.org/10.1187/cbe.16-01-0002

Schinske, Jeffrey, & Kimberly Tanner. (2014). Teaching more by grading less (or differently). *CBE—Life Sciences Education,* 13(2), 159–66. https://doi.org/10.1187/cbe.cbe-14-03-0054

Seidel, Shannon B., Amanda L. Reggi, Jeffrey N. Schinske, Laura W. Burrus, & Kimberly D. Tanner. (2015). Beyond the biology: A systematic investigation of noncontent instructor talk in an introductory biology course. *CBE—Life Sciences Education,* 14(4), Article 43. https://doi .org/10.1187/cbe.15-03-0049

Seymour, Elaine, & Nancy M. Hewitt. (1997). *Talking about leaving: Why undergraduates leave the sciences*. Westview Press.

Seymour, Elaine, & Anne-Barrie Hunter (Eds.). (2019). *Talking about leaving revisited: persistence, relocation, and loss in undergraduate STEM education*. Springer Nature.

Shapiro, Casey A., & Linda J. Sax. (December 2011). Major selection and persistence for women in STEM. *New Directions for Institutional Research,* 152, 5–18. https://doi.org/10.1002/ir.404

Sibley, Jim. (2014, October 6). *Seven mistakes to avoid when writing multiple-choice questions.* Faculty Focus. http://www.facultyfocus.com/articles /educational-assessment/seven-mistakes-avoid-writing-multiple -choice-questions/

Slakoff, Danielle. @DSlakoffPhD. (2019, September 3). *Based on @ LauraJuneDavis's brillian idea, I am rebranding "office hours" into "student hours" today* [Tweet]. Twitter. https://twitter.com/DSlakoffPhD /status/1168946177276043264

Smith, Michelle K., Francis H. M. Jones, Sarah L. Gilbert, & Carl E. Wieman. (2013, December 1). The classroom observation protocol for undergraduate STEM (COPUS): A new instrument to characterize university STEM classroom practices. *CBE—Life Sciences Education,* 12(4), 618–27. https://doi.org/10.1187/cbe.13-08-0154

Sotto-Santiago, Sylk. (2019). Time to reconsider the word minority in academic medicine. *Journal of Best Practices in Health Professions Diversity,* 12(1), 72–78.

Spurr, Kim Weaver. (2019, January 2). "Much learning and healing happened." https://college.unc.edu/2019/01/descendants-project/

Stachowiak, Bonni. (Host). (2018, October 31). Reach everyone, teach everyone. (No. 227) [Audio podcast episode]. In *Teaching in Higher Ed.* https://teachinginhighered.com/podcast/reach-everyone -teach-everyone/#transcriptcontainer

Sue, Derald Wing, Christina M. Capodilupo, Gina C. Torino, Jennifer M. Bucceri, Aisha M. B. Holder, Kevin L. Nadal, & Marta Esquilin. (2007, May). Racial microaggressions in everyday life: Implications for clinical practice. *American Psychologist,* 62(4), 271–86.

Talbert, Robert, & David Clark. (2021, October 21). *Grading for growth.* https://gradingforgrowth.substack.com

Tanner, Kimberly D. (2017). Structure matters: Twenty-one teaching strategies to promote student engagement and cultivate classroom equity. *CBE—Life Sciences Education,* 12(3), 322–31. https://doi .org/10.1187/cbe.13-06-0115

Theobald, Elli J., Mariah J. Hill, Elisa Tran, Sweta Agrawal, E. Nicole Arroyo, Shawn Behling, Nyasha Chambwe, et al. (2020, March 24). Active learning narrows achievement gaps for underrepresented students in undergraduate science, technology, engineering, and math. *Proceedings of the National Academy of Sciences,* 117(12), 6476–83. https://doi.org/10.1073/PNAS.1916903117

Tobin, Thomas J., & Kirsten T. Behling. (2018). *Reach everyone, teach everyone: Universal design for learning in higher education.* West Virginia University Press.

Tom, Gail, Stephanie Tom Tong, & Charles Hesse. (2010). Thick slice and thin slice teaching evaluations. *Social Psychology of Education,* 13(1), 129–36. https://doi.org/10.1007/s11218-009-9101-7

Treisman, U. (1992). Studying students studying calculus: A look at the lives of minority
mathematics students in college. *The College Mathematics Journal,* 23(5), 362–372. https://doi.org/10.2307/2686410

Turnbull, Jeffrey M. (2009). What is . . . normative versus criterion-referenced assessment. *Medical Teacher,* 11(2), 145–50. https://doi .org/10.3109/01421598909146317

University Gazette. (2019, March 27). *New analytics dashboard lets faculty see class demographics.* The Well. https://thewell.unc.edu/2019/03/27 /new-analytics-dashboard-lets-faculty-see-class-demographics/

University of Iowa College of Education. (2021, August.) Syllabus checklist. https://education.uiowa.edu/office-dean/policies/syllabus-checklist

University of Michigan. (n.d.). *An introduction to content warnings and*

trigger warnings. Inclusive Teaching @ U-M. https://sites.lsa
.umich.edu/inclusive-teaching/2017/12/12/an-introduction
-to-content-warnings-and-trigger-warnings/

University of Minnesota University Policy Library. (n.d.). Recommended
policy statements for syllabi. https://policy.umn.edu/education
/syllabusrequirements-appa

UNT Teaching Commons. (n.d.). *Covering content vs. uncovering content.*
https://teachingcommons.unt.edu/teaching-essentials
/student-learning/covering-content-vs-uncovering-content

Vandegrift, E. V. H., & S. M. Dawson. (2016). *Sex and gender: What does it
mean to be female or male?* CourseSource. https://doi.org/10.24918
/cs.2016.21

Waggoner Denton, Ashley, & James Veloso. (2018). Changes in syllabus
tone affect warmth (but not competence) ratings of both male and
female instructors. *Social Psychology of Education,* 21(1), 173–87.
https://doi.org/10.1007/s11218-017-9409-7

Washington University Center for Teaching and Learning. (n.d.). Syllabus
template. https://teachingcenter.wustl.edu/resources/course-design
/syllabus-template/

Waugh, Alex H., & Tessa C. Andrews. (2020). Diving into the details:
Constructing a framework of random call components. *CBE—Life
Sciences Education,* 19(2), Article 14. https://doi.org/10.1187
/cbe.19-07-0130

Weaver, Gabriela C., Ann E. Austin, Andrea Follmer Greenhoot, & Noah
D. Finkelstein. (2020, July 21). Establishing a better approach for
evaluating teaching: The TEval project. *Change: The Magazine of Higher
Learning,* 52(3), 25–31. https://doi.org/10.1080/00091383.2020
.1745575

Willingham, Daniel T. (2021). *Why don't students like school? A cognitive
scientist answers questions about how the mind works and what it means
for the classroom* (2nd ed.). Jossey-Bass.

Wood, William B., & Kimberly D. Tanner. (2012). The role of the lecturer
as tutor: Doing what effective tutors do in a large lecture class. *CBE—
Life Sciences Education,* 11(1), 3–9. https://doi.org/10.1187
/cbe.11-12-0110

Yeager, D. S., V. Purdie-Vaughns, N. Garcia, J. Apfel, P. Brzustoski, A.
Master, W. T. Hessert, M. E. Williams, & G. L. Cohen. (2013). Breaking
the cycle of mistrust: Wise interventions to provide critical feedback
across the racial divide. *Journal of Experimental Psychology: General*,
143(2), 804–24.

Zenger, Jack, & Joseph Folkman. (2016, July 14). What great listeners
actually do. *Harvard Business Review.* https://hbr.org/2016/07
/what-great-listeners-actually-do

Zipp, John F. (2007). Learning by exams: The impact of two-stage
cooperative tests. *Teaching Sociology,* 35(1), 62–76. https://doi.org
/10.1177/0092055X0703500105

INDEX

Note: page numbers in *italics* indicate illustrative material

TEACHING AND LEARNING IN HIGHER EDUCATION

Teaching Matters: A Guide for Graduate Students
Aeron Haynie and Stephanie Spong

Remembering and Forgetting in the Age of Technology:
Teaching, Learning, and the Science of Memory in a Wired World
Michelle D. Miller

Skim, Dive, Surface: Teaching Digital Reading
Jenae Cohn

Minding Bodies: How Physical Space, Sensation, and
Movement Affect Learning
Susan Hrach

Ungrading: Why Rating Students Undermines Learning
(and What to Do Instead)
Edited by Susan D. Blum

Radical Hope: A Teaching Manifesto
Kevin M. Gannon

Teaching about Race and Racism in the College Classroom:
Notes from a White Professor
Cyndi Kernahan

Intentional Tech: Principles to Guide the Use of Educational
Technology in College Teaching
Derek Bruff

Geeky Pedagogy: A Guide for Intellectuals, Introverts, and
Nerds Who Want to Be Effective Teachers
Jessamyn Neuhaus

How Humans Learn: The Science and Stories behind Effective
College Teaching
Joshua R. Eyler

Reach Everyone, Teach Everyone: Universal Design for
Learning in Higher Education
Thomas J. Tobin and Kirsten T. Behling

Teaching the Literature Survey Course: New Strategies for
College Faculty
Gwynn Dujardin, James M. Lang, and John A. Staunton

The Spark of Learning: Energizing the College Classroom
with the Science of Emotion
Sarah Rose Cavanagh